LOOM
BAND IT

LOOM
BAND IT

60 RUBBER BAND PROJECTS FOR
THE BUDDING LOOMINEER

Kat Roberts and Tessa Sillars-Powell

APPLE

A QUINTET BOOK

First published in the UK in 2014 by Apple Press
74-77 White Lion Street,
London N1 9PF
United Kingdom

www.apple-press.com

ISBN: 978-1-84543-563-9

QTT.LOOB

Conceived, designed, and produced by
Quintet Publishing Limited
114-116 Western Road
Hove, East Sussex
BN3 1DD
United Kingdom

Project Editor: Caroline Elliker
Design: Maria Mokina
Photography: Simon Pask and Gareth Butterworth
Illustrations: Gareth Butterworth
Art Director: Michael Charles
Managing Editor: Emma Bastow
Publisher: Mark Searle

Printed in China by 1010 Printing International Ltd

Date of manufacture: May 2014

9 8 7 6 5 4 3 2 1

CONTENTS

INTRODUCTION

GETTING TO KNOW YOUR LOOM

If you're new to looming, it's useful to know some handy tips to get you started. There are always going to be different ways of doing things, and once you've picked up the basics you'll begin to find your own looming style and develop new techniques. It's amazing how quickly your confidence can grow with a little bit of patience – be prepared to discover the endless possibilities of your loom, while having lots of fun using it!

EQUIPMENT AND MATERIALS

In order to complete most of the projects in this book, there is some basic equipment you will need:

Loom: Other looms are available, but this book focuses on designs and methods achievable on the Rainbow Loom®.

Hook: You can use the one that comes with the Rainbow Loom® or alternatively use a crochet hook. Crochet hooks are generally stronger if you are hooking a lot of tight bands at one time.

Rubber Bands: These are available in a wide variety of colours, but be sure to use good quality ones, as this will affect the stretch and finish of your design.

Clips: You'll need them to finish off some of the projects. They come in many different shapes and sizes and are either plastic or metal. They are readily available at most band stockists. C-clips are small, plastic clips, shaped like the letter "C", and are the most common.

S-clips and O-clips are variations of these, and can be used in the same way.

Scissors: Occasionally, it's necessary to snip off excess bands. You can snap them, but it's easier to cut them.

Pliers: You may need these when working with metal jewellery attachments.

Metal jewellery rings: These are the rings used to link more traditional jewellery. They are a bit more durable than plastic clips and ensure your projects stay together longer. To use

them, you'll need a pair of pliers. Bend out one end, slide the bands inside and secure close using pliers.

For certain designs you may need additional items, such as hair bands and beads; these are listed at the start of the instructions.

When choosing beads, try to find ones with holes big enough to thread your bands through. Exciting beads can really set off some of these projects and turn them into special jewellery pieces that nobody else will have.

Earring hooks, brooch pins and hair clips are useful for turning your charms into more wearable pieces, and they are available from most craft shops.

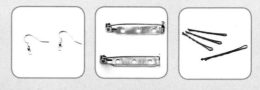

SETTING UP YOUR LOOM

There are a few different ways of setting up your loom. The two most common are 'Staggered' and 'Squared'. In this book it will always say which method  you need to use, and it's important to check this before placing your bands.

In the Staggered configuration, the pegs are offset. Do this by unclipping the central row, moving it down, and clipping it back as shown in the diagram.

In the Squared configuration, the pegs are aligned at right angles. Do this by unclipping the central row, moving it up, and clipping it back as shown in the diagram.

As you work through the book, there may be times when it is useful to attach two looms together. There is often a way of getting around this with one loom, and if so, we'll tell you how. To attach two looms, move the blue connectors  up to where the join will be and simply clip both looms into the connector. You can either go long ways, or side by side.

It's vital to ensure the arrows on the pegs are facing the right direction before you start placing your bands. In the more unusual projects, be aware that it might be necessary to have the arrows in different rows facing different directions.

LAYING THE LOOM

For each project in this book there's a simple diagram showing you how to lay all the bands before you start your looping. It's important to follow the numbers on these; if the bands aren't laid in the correct order you may get into difficulty later. Some of the designs have multiple diagrams to demonstrate variations, but feel free to substitute colours at any point to customise your creations and stand out from the crowd.

To get great outcomes, make sure your bands aren't twisted when placing them on the loom. Something so simple can make a noticeable difference and distinguish an amateur from a pro!

Occasionally, it may be necessary to double-over a band. To do this, stretch it  over one of the pegs, pull back, twist it and loop back over the pegs making it twice as tight. This technique will be shown in the diagram with two lines.

Topper bands (sometimes referred to as cap bands) feature in several designs and hold everything together, so pay attention to where they appear. To create  them, take a standard band and simply loop and wrap it around the required peg twice.

Sometimes, it may need to be wrapped more than twice, and the instructions will tell you if this is the case.

LOOPING THE LOOM

Hooking bands is the key skill to learn. In the majority of these designs, the hooking happens from within the peg. This means that once you've looped a band to its destination it generally carries other bands with it in its loop, creating a chain or link. Understanding this principle will allow you to see any potential errors before removing your project from the loom, saving you a lot of time!

It therefore makes quite a difference which way you hook, so always check the instructions to see which way it states. If you are hooking from the inside, put your hook facing forwards into the peg, use the back of your hook to push back any other bands and catch the required band.

Sometimes you will be required to hook outside the pegs, so be aware of this also.

LOOPING OFF

When you get to the end of the loom there are a few different ways of finishing off.
C-clips: Most common and easy to use, they can attach multiple bands together. Tightly pull the bands you wish to link and slide them through the gap in the C-clip. S-clips and O-clips can be used in the same way.

Slipknots: These are really simple and great for ensuring a lot of bands remain together. To make one, put your hook through the finishing peg, so that it pokes out of the bottom. Place a band on the hook and pull tight. Keeping hold of the other end of the band, pull your hook up inside the peg and out of the top. Loop the other end of the band (that you are still holding) onto the hook, over the end already on the hook. Finally, pull the end you originally hooked off the hook and pull it tight. This will create a slipknot.

Extending: Sometimes it might be necessary to extend a bracelet, which you can do with a simple chain. First, scoop all of the bands on your last peg onto the stem of your hook. Take another band, put one end on the hook, and pull the other tight. Slide the bands from the stem of your hook onto the new band.

Put both ends of the new band onto the stem of your hook. Continue pulling new bands through in this style until the design reaches your desired length. Finish off by putting the last two ends through a C-clip.

THE MINI LOOM

The Mini Loom is a great piece of equipment to learn how to use. It comes in

every Rainbow Loom® kit, and is the small blue piece. Because of its size, it's handy for when you are on the go, so you never need be without a loom! There are a number of cool designs you can achieve with it, and you'll find a few projects in this book.

One of its main benefits is that you don't need to spend any time laying the bands; you just add them as you go, so you can work quite quickly with it. It's also really useful when you want to extend an existing bracelet.

Stretch the last link in the chain between the two pegs, and put your hook through one of them. Catch a new band on the end of your hook. Pull it through, and loop the other end of the band onto the hook, too. Catch another new band, pull it through the links of the last band, and loop the other end of it onto the hook. Repeat this until you are happy with the length and finish off with a C-clip.

TOP TIPS

- Keep your work area neat. This will save you time and allow you to work more efficiently.

- Make sure you have all the bands you need for a project before starting to lay the loom; there's nothing more frustrating than running out!

- Be patient. If the bands get tangled when looping, don't give up straight away. Often, if you look carefully, you can work out where you went wrong and easily fix the error. If not, don't be put off attempting it again – practise makes perfect!

- Have the confidence to adapt the designs and experiment by changing the colours to really personalise your creations.

- Have fun!

PROJECT SELECTOR

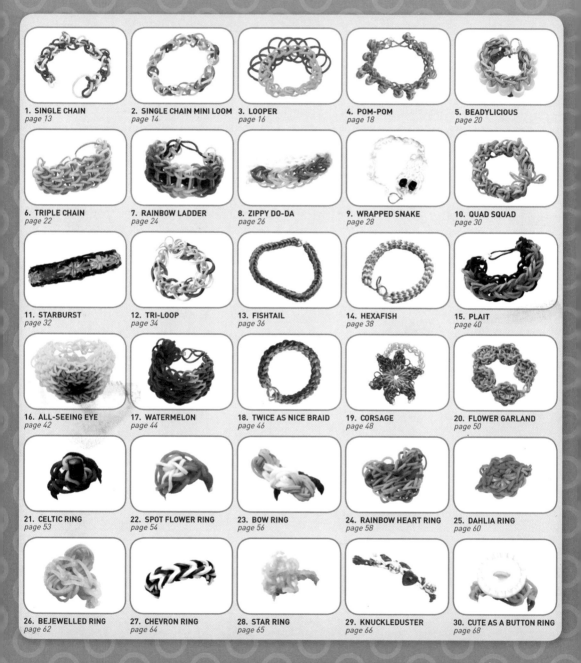

1. SINGLE CHAIN
page 13

2. SINGLE CHAIN MINI LOOM
page 14

3. LOOPER
page 16

4. POM-POM
page 18

5. BEADYLICIOUS
page 20

6. TRIPLE CHAIN
page 22

7. RAINBOW LADDER
page 24

8. ZIPPY DO-DA
page 26

9. WRAPPED SNAKE
page 28

10. QUAD SQUAD
page 30

11. STARBURST
page 32

12. TRI-LOOP
page 34

13. FISHTAIL
page 36

14. HEXAFISH
page 38

15. PLAIT
page 40

16. ALL-SEEING EYE
page 42

17. WATERMELON
page 44

18. TWICE AS NICE BRAID
page 46

19. CORSAGE
page 48

20. FLOWER GARLAND
page 50

21. CELTIC RING
page 53

22. SPOT FLOWER RING
page 54

23. BOW RING
page 56

24. RAINBOW HEART RING
page 58

25. DAHLIA RING
page 60

26. BEJEWELLED RING
page 62

27. CHEVRON RING
page 64

28. STAR RING
page 65

29. KNUCKLEDUSTER
page 66

30. CUTE AS A BUTTON RING
page 68

31. HOOPLA EARRINGS
page 71

32. BOW TIE
page 72

33. PENCIL GRIP
page 74

34. HOT DRINKS HOLDER
page 76

35. SKATER BELT
page 78

36. BAREFOOT SANDAL
page 80

37. TIARA
page 82

38. CAT EARS
page 84

39. GLASSES SLEEVE
page 86

40. PEARL NECKLACE
page 88

41. UNICORN
page 91

42. BUG
page 94

43. CUPCAKE
page 96

44. STRAWBERRY
page 98

45. BUMBLEBEE
page 99

46. SNAIL
page 100

47. BUTTERFLY
page 102

48. OCTOPUS
page 104

49. SKATEBOARD
page 106

50. FLOWER POWER
page 108

51. RAINBOW
page 109

52. CACTUS
page 110

53. BIRTHDAY GIFT
page 113

54. VALENTINE'S HEART
page 114

55. EASTER BUNNY
page 116

56. ALOHA NECKLACE
page 118

57. HALLOWEEN SPIDER
page 120

58. FIREWORKS NECKLACE
page 122

59. SNOWFLAKE
page 124

60. CHRISTMAS STOCKING
page 126

CHAPTER 1
BRILLIANT BRACELETS

Bracelets are a really cool thing to learn to make. There are so many variations and unusual patterns that you can create on your loom; the possibilities are endless! Experiment by changing the colours. Personalise them to your favourite team or make matching ones for your best friends. Nothing says 'friends forever' like a unique band bracelet! In this chapter, there are a selection of designs to work from, varying in complexity. If you're a beginner, try some of the simpler patterns first, before diving in. Once you've got the basics, there'll be no stopping you!

1. SINGLE CHAIN

Loom configuration: STAGGERED

You will need
8 blue
8 red
8 white
1 C-clip

Place the loom with the arrows facing away from you and lay the bands as per the diagram.

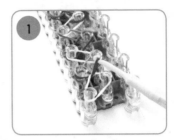

1. Turn the loom so the arrow is facing down towards you. Place your hook through the first central peg and loop the bottom band to its original peg, on the upper left-hand side.

2. Put your hook through the peg you just finished on and loop the bottom band to its original peg on the upper right-hand side.

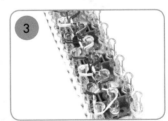

3. Repeat this process to the end of the loom.

4. Put your hook through the final peg and attach the two ends of the last band with a C-clip.

5. Pull off the loom and link the other end of the bracelet into the C-clip.

2. SINGLE CHAIN MINI LOOM

Loom configuration: MINI LOOM

You will need
6 pink
6 purple
6 yellow
6 green
1 C-clip

This is a really simple way of creating a bracelet with the same finish as the single chain, but on the Mini Loom.

1. Stretch a single band twice around the two pegs of your Mini Loom. The band should sit in the groove of the pegs.

2. Put your hook down through the sideways groove, and, holding on to the bottom end of your next band, catch its top end onto the hook.

JSYK!

The Mini Loom is perfect for when you're on the go and need to loom in a hurry. See page 9 for more information.

3. Pull your hook back up through the groove and then loop the bottom end of the band onto the hook, too.

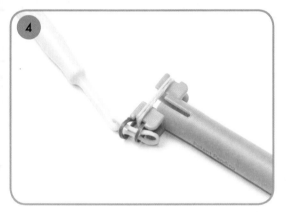

4. Catch your next colored band on the hook and pull it through the two loops of the band on the hook. To make this easier, turn your hook so it faces downwards.

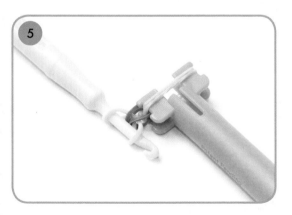

5. Loop the bottom end of the new band onto the hook as well.

6. Keep repeating steps 4 and 5 until your chain reaches the desired length, or you have used all the bands. Then, slide a C-clip to link the last two ends together.

7. Pull off the Mini Loom and link the other end of the chain into the C-clip, too.

3. LOOPER

Loom configuration: STAGGERED

You will need

20 yellow
9 red
1 C-clip

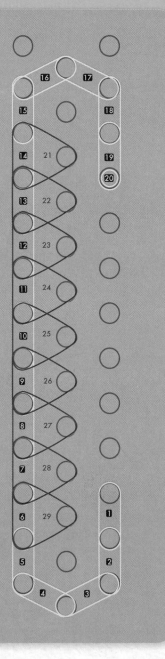

Turn the loom so that the arrow is facing away from you. Loop bands 1–20 according to the provided layout. Band number 20 will be a topper band.

1. Turn the loom around so the arrows are now facing you. Beginning at the peg with band 20 on it, insert your hook into the peg, pull away the topper band to hook the band beneath it, and loop it backward onto the peg it started from. Continue looping from one band to the next.

4. Remove your bracelet from the loom and connect the C-clip to the end with the topper band.

5. When you first remove the bracelet from the loom, the red bands may look a little bit strange. Take a moment to arrange them by gently pulling them down a bit.

2. When you reach a peg with a red band around it, insert the hook into the peg to push it away. Hook the band beneath it and continue.

3. When you reach the last peg put a C-clip on those bands.

4. POM-POM

Loom configuration: STAGGERED

You will need

25 orange
12 turquoise
12 pink
1 C-clip

To make the pom-poms

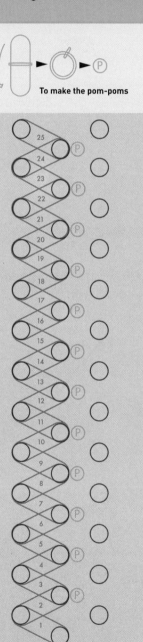

Place the loom with the arrows facing away from you and lay the orange bands as per the diagram.

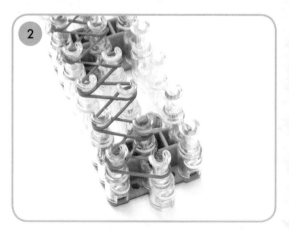

1. It's now time to make those pom-poms! Take a pink band, and wrap it around your hook three times. Hook a blue band, pull it tight, and slide the pink band on to it.

2. Loop both ends of the blue band over the pegs marked with a 'P' in the diagram on the left. Repeat this eleven times more so each 'P' peg has a pom-pom on it.

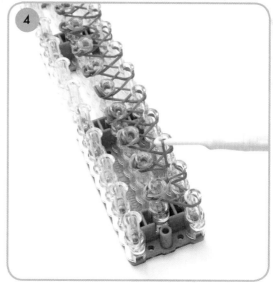

3. Turn the loom so the arrow is facing down towards you. This is the same method as the single chain. Place your hook through the bottom central peg and loop the bottom band to the peg located just up, and to the right. Then put your hook through the peg you just finished on and loop the bottom band to its original peg on the upper right-hand side.

4. Repeat this process to the end of the loom.

5. Put your hook through the final peg and attach the two ends of the last band with a C-clip.

6. Pull off the loom and link the other end of the bracelet into the C-clip.

FYI!

If you enjoy cheerleading, attract even more attention by matching your pom-pom colours to your bracelet colours!

BEADYLICIOUS

Loom configuration: **STAGGERED**

You will need

28 blue
11 pink
1 C-clip
11 beads

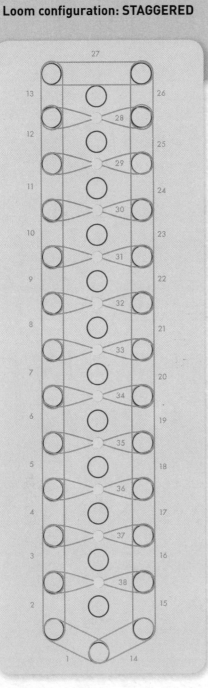

Place the loom with the arrows facing away from you and lay the bands as per the diagram. Topper band 27 is wrapped twice around the pegs. When laying pink bands 28–38, thread them through a single bead before stretching between the pegs.

1. Turn the loom so the arrow is facing down towards you. Put your hook inside the first left-hand peg, push back the topper band, hook the bottom blue band, and loop it forward.

J4F!

Why not try arranging the beads in rainbow colours for variation?

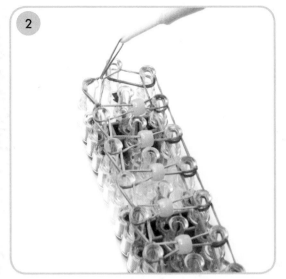

2. Continue looping like this for the next 12 bands in this row. Always hook from inside the pink bands. The last band in the chain will be looped diagonally to the top central peg.

4. Put your hook in the top central peg, catch your finishing blue band to the end of it, pull it through, and create a slipknot.

5. Pull your beady bracelet off the loom, and attach the two ends using a C-clip. If you need to make it slightly longer, see page 8 to learn how to extend your bracelet by adding extra links.

3. Repeat steps 1 and 2 on the right-hand side.

6. TRIPLE CHAIN

Loom configuration: STAGGERED

You will need

18 pink
18 green
13 orange
C-clip

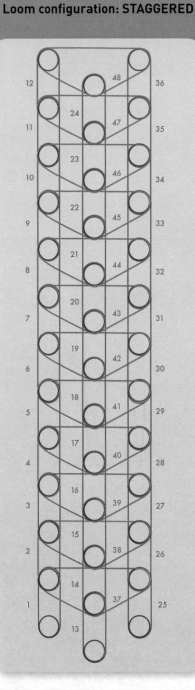

Place the loom with the arrows facing away from you and lay the bands as per the diagram.

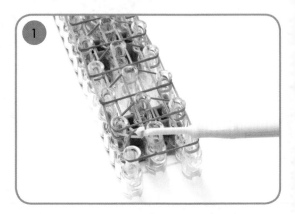

1. Turn the loom so the arrow is facing down towards you. Place your hook down through the first left-hand peg, hook the bottom green band, and loop forward to the peg in front.

2. Put your hook through the second left-hand peg, hook the bottom pink band, and loop forward to the peg in front. Continue to loop the left-hand side up to the end of the loom, each time making sure that you are putting your hook through the inside of the peg to collect the bands, rather than the outside!

FYI!

This one is a little more complex, and best attempted after you have mastered the art of the Single Chain Bracelet on page 13.

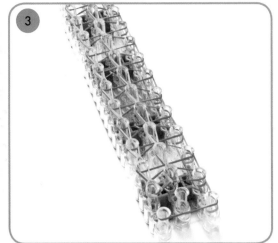

3. Repeat the process with the middle row of pegs.

5. Put your hook through the last peg in the right-hand row and loop both ends of the band over to the last central peg. Repeat on the left-hand side.

4. Then, work on the right-hand side. The first orange band should be evenly stretched between the three rows of pegs.

6. Put your hook through the last central peg, hook, and pull your finishing band through all the other bands before looping through itself in a slipknot. Pull off the loom and attach the two ends with a C-clip.

7. RAINBOW LADDER

Loom configuration: STAGGERED

You will need

14 black	8 red
8 green	8 orange
8 blue	6 yellow
8 purple	1 C-clip

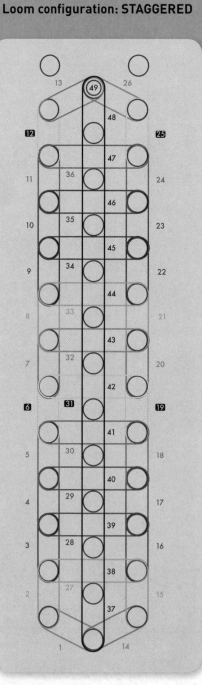

Place the loom with the arrows facing away from you and lay bands 1–49 as per the diagram. You should still have two each of the blue, purple, red, and orange plus one of the yellow and green left. We'll place them after the first two steps.

1. Turn the loom around so the arrows are pointing down towards you. Starting at the bottom central peg, put your hook in, push back the topper band, and catch the first band beneath it (shown in black). Loop it forward to the peg in front.

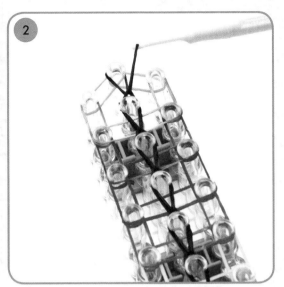

2. Continue looping the black bands to the end of the loom, ending on the top central peg.

3. Now we need to lay the rest of the bands. On top of each of the 'rungs' of the ladder, stretch an additional band in the same colour as the existing one between the two opposite pegs.

4. Back to the looping, make sure the arrows are still pointing down towards you, put your hook in the bottom central peg, and using the back of it to push back the topper band, catch the bottom-left green band. Loop it to its original peg on the upper left-hand side. Continue looping the bands on the left-hand side, making sure each time that you hook from the inside of the peg.

5. Repeat this process for the right-hand side row of pegs.

6. Put your hook through the peg you just ended on, and pull the finishing band through and over itself in a slipknot. It is ready to pull off the loom! Attach both ends using the C-clip.

8. ZIPPY DO-DA

Loom configuration: STAGGERED

You will need
26 yellow
10 purple
10 green
1 C-clip

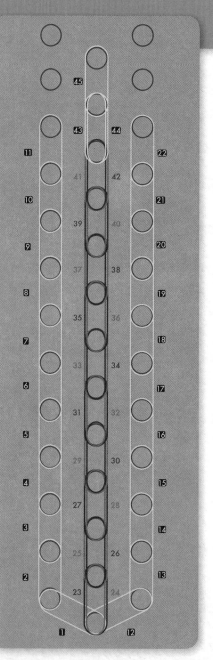

Place the loom with the arrows facing away from you and lay the bands as per the diagram.

1. Turn the loom so the arrow is facing down toward you. Put your hook through the second central peg from the bottom, hook the top band, and loop it to the upper left-hand peg. Repeat by taking the next band from the central peg to the right-hand side.

2. Go to the bottom peg on the left-hand side, put your hook through the center of it to hook the bottom band, and loop it forward. Repeat on the right-hand side.

3. Put your hook through the third central peg from the bottom, hook the second band from the bottom, and loop it to the upper left-hand peg. Repeat on the right side.

4. Repeat this looping pattern to the end of the loom using the diagram on page 27 as a reminder: 3 is always the top band and 4 the bottom. Make sure that you hook from inside the peg each time.

26

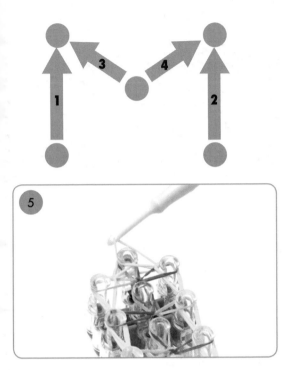

OVER THE RAINBOW

You will need

26 white	4 green
4 purple	4 blue
4 red	1 C-clip
4 orange	
4 yellow	

5. Through the last peg on the left-hand side, hook the bottom band to the top central peg. Repeat on the right-hand side.

6. Finally, put your hook through the top central peg, loop your finishing band through to create a slipknot, and pull off the loom! Attach both ends with a C-clip.

9. WRAPPED SNAKE

Loom configuration: STAGGERED

You will need

45 white
1 pink
2 beads
1 C-clip

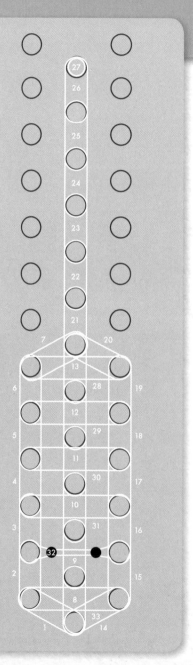

Place the loom with the arrows facing away from you and lay bands as per diagram. The band at position 32 will have the two black beads strung onto it before being placed. Once on the pegs, push one of the beads to the left side and the other bead to the right side. When you are placing the bands you will still have 12 white bands and one pink band left over, to be be used later. These will form a chain of bands looped in a simple zig-zag design to add length to the bracelet.

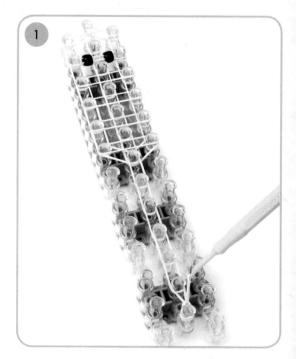

1. Turn the loom so that the arrows are facing you. Begin at the bottom central peg by inserting your hook into it to push away the topper band. Hook the band beneath it and pull it onto the peg in front of it.

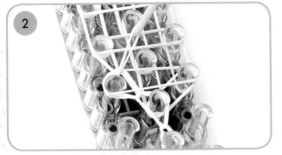

2. Continue looping the bands onto the peg they originated from. Whenever you come across a peg that has a horizontal band stretched across it, insert your hook into the peg to push those bands back before hooking the band beneath it.

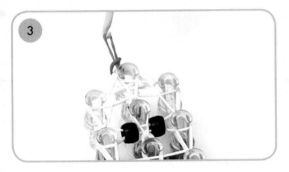

3. When you get to the final peg, insert your hook through the peg to the bottom. Use your pink band to make a slipknot for the tongue. Put a C-clip onto the end of the pink band and remove the snake from the loom.

4. Now we are going to make an extra chain of bands to lengthen the tail. With the loom arrows facing away from you, place the remaining bands in a zig-zag pattern as per the Single Chain Bracelet design on page 13. Place the topper band from the snake's tail over band 12.

5. Turn the loom so the arrows are facing you. Insert the hook into the bottom peg, pulling back the topper band from the snake tail, to hook the band beneath it. Loop that band forward.

6. Continue looping forward. When you get to the last peg, secure those bands with a slipknot using the last white band.

7. Tie two or three knots into the loose end of the slipknot to make it look more like the end of a tail.

8. From the knotted slipknot, count up seven bands and put the other side of the C-clip on it.

10. QUAD SQUAD

Loom configuration: STAGGERED

You will need
14 pink
12 blue
12 orange
12 green
1 C-clip

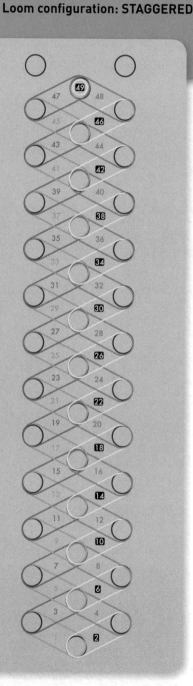

Place loom with the arrows facing away from you and lay the bands. Don't forget pink topper band 49!

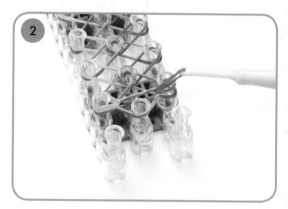

1. Turn the loom so the arrow is facing down toward you. Put your hook through the topper band of the first central peg, hook the band second from bottom (shown in green), and loop it to its original peg on the upper left-hand side.

2. Put your hook back through the first central peg to loop the bottom band (shown in orange) over to its original peg on the upper right-hand side.

5. Put your hook through the top central peg, hook your finishing band through the bands, and then through itself to create a slipknot. Pull off the loom and attach the two ends with a C-clip.

3. As per the diagram on the right, put your hook through the second peg up on the left-hand side to catch the bottom band (shown in pink) and loop it to the second central peg up.

4. Repeat this looping pattern to the end of the loom, using the diagram on the right for guidance.

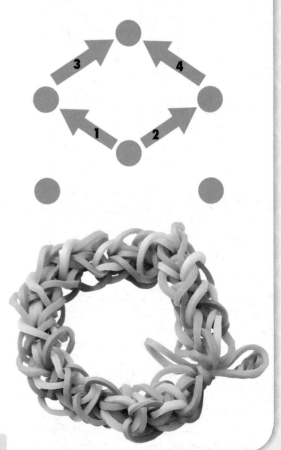

11. STARBURST

Loom configuration: STAGGERED

You will need

28 black
7 red
7 orange
7 yellow
7 green
7 blue
7 purple
1 C-clip

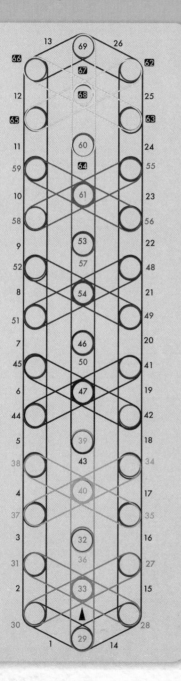

Place the loom with the arrows facing away from you and lay the bands. Don't forget the twice-wrapped topper bands: 33, 40, 47, 54, 61, 68, 69!

1. Turn the loom so the arrow is facing down toward you. Place your hook through the center of the first star, inside the peg. Using the back of your hook, push back the topper band, hook the first band, and loop it to its original peg.

2. Repeat this step with the remaining five bands, working in an anticlockwise direction. The topper band should then be evenly stretched around the central peg.

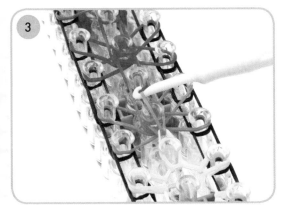

3. Moving on to the next star, start by hooking the band in the six o'clock position upwards to the central peg. It will lie on top of the topper band.

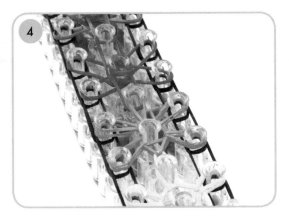

4. Put your hook through the star's central peg. Using the back of your peg, push back the topper band, hook the top band, and loop it back to its original peg. Repeat this for the remaining bands in this star.

5. Repeat steps 3 and 4 for the remaining four stars.

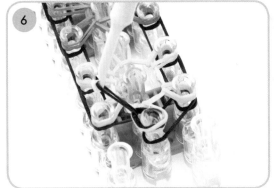

6. Starting at the first central peg, put your hook through it and take the second band from the bottom to its original peg on the upper left-hand side. Repeat all the way up the left-hand side until the last band comes onto the top central peg.

7. Repeat step 6 up the right-hand side, from bottom central to top central peg.

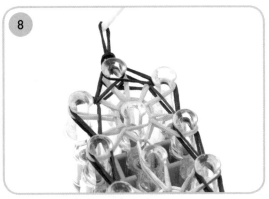

8. Put your hook through the top central peg, loop a band to its tip, and pull through to create a slipknot. Pull your starburst bracelet off the loom, attach the ends together with a C-clip, and wear to dazzle all your friends!

FTW!

Try making this one with alternate coloured stars. You could make it to match your favourite team, and recreate it for all your friends. Nothing says team spirit like matching bracelets!

12. TRI-LOOP

Loom configuration: **SQUARED, MIDDLE ROW IN REVERSE**

You will need

25 yellow
18 blue
15 white
1 C-clip

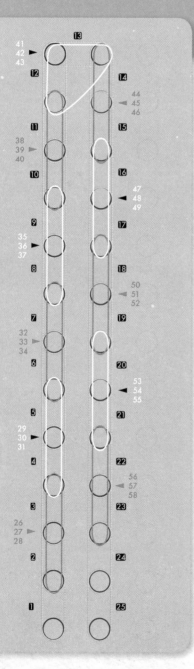

Before laying the loom, remove the middle row and turn it around so the arrows face the opposite direction to the other two rows. Make sure that the middle row arrows are facing toward you and lay the bands as per the diagram, in the numbered order.

1. Keeping the loom with the middle row arrows pointing towards you, put your hook in the second central peg, pick up the bottom band, and loop it forward to the peg in front.

5. Once you get to the end of the row, attach the two ends of the last band with a C-clip, pull off the loom, and slide in the other end of the bracelet.

2. Put your hook inside the next central peg, pick up the bottom band, and loop it forward to the peg in front. Keep doing this to the end of the row.

3. At the last peg, take the bottom band from inside and loop it to the left-hand peg.

4. Turn the loom so the arrows in the middle row are facing away from you and continue to loop the yellow bands up what is now the right-hand row. Remember to always hook the bottom band from the inside.

IU2U!

Try experimenting with different colours to make an Olympic-themed bracelet!

13. FISHTAIL

Loom configuration: ONLY REQUIRES 2 PEGS

You will need

29 orange
29 purple
2 'spare' bands
1 C-clip

With this design, you'll be hooking from the outside of the pegs. Choose two pegs that are side by side to start on.

1. Take your first rubber band, hook it over the first peg, twist it once, and put it onto the adjacent peg, making a figure 8.

FYEO!

Why not match the fishtail bracelet with a fishtail braid in your hair? It's a really elegant design that's simple to achieve.

2. Now, without twisting it, put a contrasting band around the two pegs and place a further band, the same colour as the original, on top of these without twisting.

3. Hook the bottom band from the right-hand side of the twist over the right-hand peg. Repeat with the left-hand side of the twist over the leg peg. The bottom band is now off the pegs, suspended around the two remaining bands.

5. Repeat step 3, looping the bottom band first off the right-hand peg and then over the left, to suspend it over the remaining bands. Add another contrasting band, and loop the bottom band up off the pegs and over it. Keep doing this with the remaining bands, using your two 'spare' bands last.

6. Put your C-clip around the ends of the last looped band, bring up the bottom end of the bracelet, and link through the clip, too.

7. Take the bracelet off the loom and pull out the two spare bands.

4. Stretch another contrasting-coloured band between the two pegs, above the others.

14. HEXAFISH

Loom configuration: SQUARED

You will need

30 orange
30 turquoise
30 white
1 C-clip

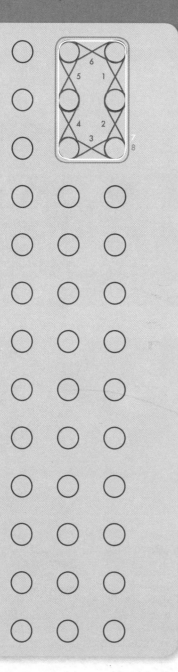

Lay the first eight bands in figure 8s as shown.

1. Starting at the top left peg, hook the two bottom bands from the outside and loop over the top of the peg to rest in the middle.

2. Repeat step 1 in a clockwise direction for the remaining five pegs.

3. Stretch a band in the same colour as the first band (shown in orange) over the six pegs, to form a rectangle.

4. At the top left peg, hook the bottom band from the outside and loop it over the top of the peg to rest in the middle. Repeat this step, moving in a clockwise direction for the remaining five pegs.

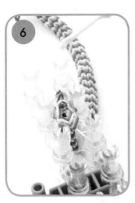

5. Repeat steps 3 and 4 until you have the length required. Keep pulling tight through the bottom of the loom as you alternate your colors. The final time, loop both bottom bands over pegs so only one remains on each peg.

6. Now, using the hook, move the band from the top left-hand peg to the top right-hand peg.

7. Move the bands from the second right-hand peg to the second left hand peg. Now move all the bands from the third left-hand peg to the third right-hand peg.

8. Take a band in the next colour of the pattern and stretch it between the three pegs with the bands on to topper them.

9. In turn, hook all the bands from each peg from the outside and loop over the top of the peg so they are suspended in the middle by the most recent topper band.

10. Carefully hook all three ends of the topper band onto one peg. Put your hook through the center of the same peg, catch a finishing band, pull it through, and loop it back on itself to create a slipknot. Take this end off the loom.

11. Find the six bands at the other end and stretch them over a single peg. Cut off the six loose bands. Put your hook through the center of this peg; loop another finishing band up through and onto itself to make a slipknot. Attach the two ends with a C-clip.

15. PLAIT

Loom configuration: STAGGERED

You will need
12 orange
12 purple
28 black
1 C-clip

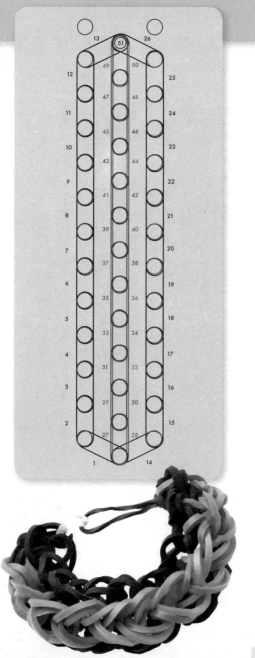

Place the loom with the arrows facing away from you and lay the bands as per the diagram.

1. Turn the loom so the arrow is facing down towards you. Put your hook through the first central peg and loop the bottom two bands forward.

2. Putting your hook back through the first central peg, push back the topper band, catch the second-to-bottom band, and loop its original peg on the upper left-hand side.

3. Repeat this step by putting your hook in the first central peg, pushing back the topper band, and looping the bottom band to its original peg on the upper right-hand side.

4. Put your hook through the second peg up on the left-hand side and loop the bottom band forward. Repeat on the right-hand side.

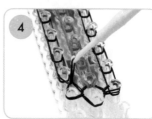

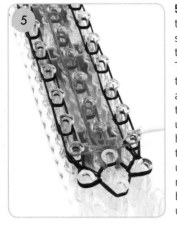

5. Put your hook through the second peg up in the central row. Take the second-to-bottom band and loop it over to the peg on the upper left. Put your hook back through the second peg up in the central row, and take the bottom band to the upper right.

6. Repeat steps 4 and 5 using the diagram below to help, until the end of the loom.

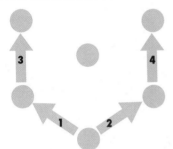

VARIATION

SWEETHEART PLAIT

You will need
28 white
12 red
12 pink
1 C-clip

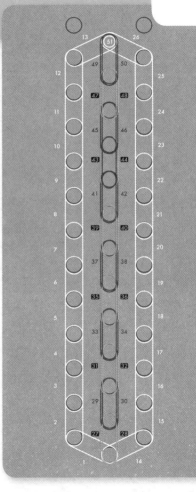

7. With the final bands of the right- and left-hand rows, instead of looping them forward as you would with the previous pegs, put your hook inside the peg and loop the bottom band to the top central peg.

8. Put your hook through the top central peg, catch a finishing band through to make a slipknot with itself, and pull off the loom. Attach both ends with the C-clip.

16. ALL-SEEING EYE

Loom configuration: 2 LOOMS, SQUARED

You will need

111 white
32 blue
5 black
4 C-clips

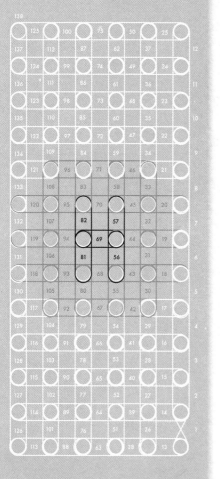

Place the looms with the arrows facing away from you. Start on the bottom left corner. Twist the first band into a figure 8 and stretch between the pegs. Lay the rest of the bands in the diagram in numerical order. Don't forget topper band 138.

1. Turn the looms around so the arrows are now facing you. You will now loop all of the bands in the reverse order. Start with the band in the bottom right corner, beneath the topper band. Hook it from inside the peg and onto the peg in front of it. Continue doing this, until you reach the end of the row.

2. When you reach the end of the row, return to the bottom right and begin looping each horizontal band from right to left. Do this to the rest of the horizontal bands in this row.

6. Turn the loom so the arrows are facing you. Insert the hook into the peg, pushing back the topper band and hooking onto the band beneath it. Loop it forward on the band in front of it.

7. Put a C-clip on the last band and remove the strap from the loom. Repeat these steps to make the second strap.

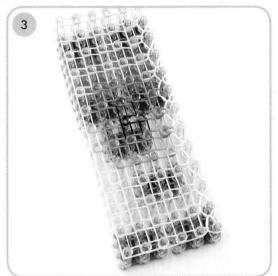

3. Repeat looping on all of the other rows, vertical followed by horizontal, moving from right to left.

4. When you get back to the peg at the far left corner add a C-clip to it. Also add a C-clip to the bands at the top right corner. Now unhook your project.

8. Attach the side of the strap with the C-clip to the bottom right corner of your bracelet and hook the end with the topper band to the C-clip on the top right corner. Repeat on the top corners with the other strap on the left side.

5. To make the straps, start by going back to a single loom with a staggered configuration with the arrows facing away from you, and use the Single Chain Bracelet diagram on page 13 to place the bands. Begin to loop one band at a time back to the peg it started on in a zig-zag pattern.

17. WATERMELON

Loom configuration: 2 LOOMS, STAGGERED

You will need

39 red
23 green
10 black
6 light green
1 C-clip

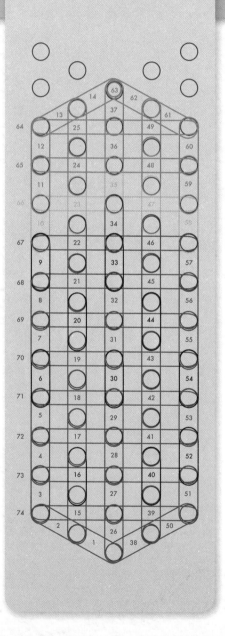

Turn the looms so that the arrow is facing away from you. Loop bands 1–62 according to the provided layout. Band number 63 will be a topper band. Set aside six light green bands, as these will be used later to make a strap.

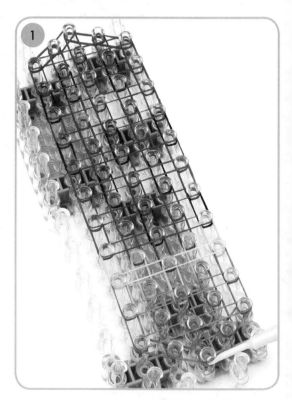

1. Turn the looms around so the arrows are now facing you. Beginning at the bottom central peg, start looming the vertical bands in the reverse order that you laid them. The horizontal bands will remain in the same position the entire time. Start by inserting the hook into the bottom central peg to push the topper band back and hook onto the band beneath.

4. When you have reached the last peg, hook all of the bands on it with a C-clip and remove the project from the looms.

2. Pull up and off the peg, stretching it back to the peg it started from.

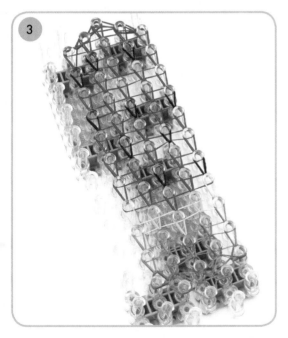

5. To make the strap, turn one loom with arrows facing away from you and lay the remaining bands over the loom as shown. Place the topper band of the project over the last peg.

6. Insert the hook into the peg, looping each band on the peg it originated from. When you get to the last one, gently unhook it from the loom and attach the bands from that peg onto the other side of the C-clip.

3. Keep looping forward in this way, making sure that you take the bottom band from inside the peg each time. Once you get to the end of the row, loop the last band to the top central peg. Continue on to the next band working down the left side, the three center rows, then the right side. There are a lot of bands in this project, so refer back to the diagram whenever you need to remember which band comes next.

18. TWICE AS NICE BRAID

Loom configuration: 2 LOOMS, 2 ROWS, STAGGERED

You will need

52 purple
50 orange
1 C-clip

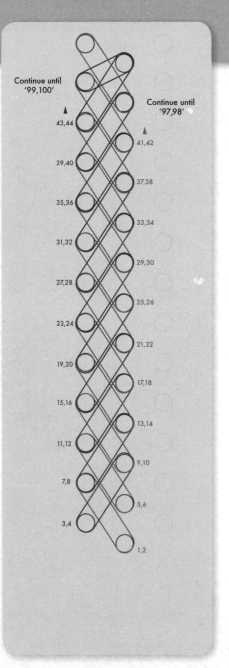

Continue until '99,100'

43,44

39,40

35,36

31,32

27,28

23,24

19,20

15,16

11,12

7,8

3,4

Continue until '97,98'

41,42

37,38

33,34

29,30

25,26

21,22

17,18

13,14

9,10

5,6

1,2

Place the loom with the arrows facing away from you and lay the bands as per the diagram. NOTE: Bands are put on the loom in pairs for this design.

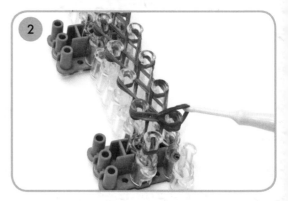

1. Turn the loom so the arrow is facing down towards you. Put your hook by the first right-hand peg and hook the pair of bands to their original peg, the second one up on the left.

2. At the first peg on the left-hand side, hook the top pair of bands to their original peg, the second one up on the right.

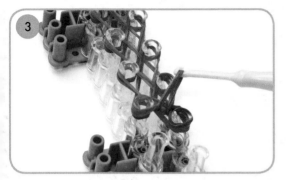

3. Now, back at the first peg on the left-hand side, loop the pair of bands to their original peg, the third one up on the right.

4. Put your hook through the inside of second peg on the right, get the pair of bands from the bottom, and loop them to their original peg, the third up on the left.

5. Put your hook through the inside of the second peg up on the left, get the pair of bands from the bottom, and loop them to their original peg.

6. Repeat steps 4 and 5, zig-zagging your way from right to left to the end of the loom, making sure each time that you hook the bottom bands from inside the peg. Check that your bands make this pattern.

7. Once you've looped all the bands, carefully move all the bands from the top two pegs on the left-hand side to the top right-hand peg. It will be very tight, so support your hook with your fingers to prevent it from breaking.

8. Put your hook through the top right-hand peg, and use your last pair of purple bands to make a slipknot (by doubling them, they will be extra strong). Pull off the loom and attach both ends using a C-clip.

FYI!

If using one loom, make half the bracelet, and extend. Lay the loom as diagram, but instead of 97 and 98 place bands 45 and 46 and instead of 99 and 100 place 47 and 48.

19. CORSAGE

Loom configuration: STAGGERED

You will need

66 purple
30 pink
1 orange
24 green
7 C-clip

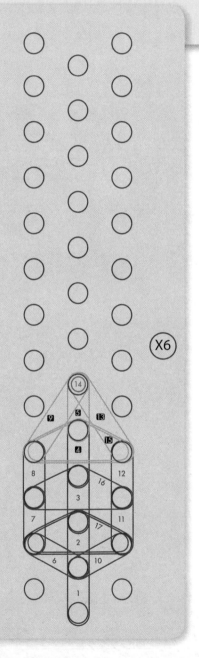

(X6)

Place the loom with the arrows facing away from you and lay the bands as per the diagram.
NOTE: You are going to lay the loom like this a total of six times, to create six petals. Topper band 14 is wrapped twice around the peg.

1. Turn the loom so the arrow is facing down toward you. Put your hook in the first central peg, push back the topper band, hook the first band down, and loop it diagonally to the upper left-hand side.

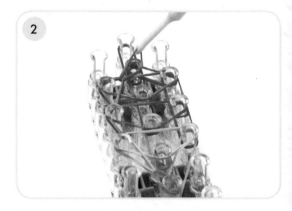

2. Continue looping forward the next three bands in this row. The last band will be looped diagonally to the upper central peg.

3. Repeat steps 1 and 2 on the right-hand side.

4. Put your hook back in the first central peg, take the last band, and loop it forward to the peg in front. Repeat looping in this row for the next three bands.

5. Put your hook in the peg you just finished, reach down and catch the bottom band, loop it forward, and join both ends of it together with a C-clip. Pull your first petal off the loom.

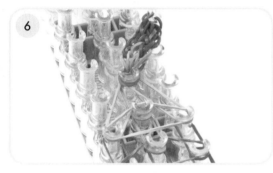

6. Relay the loom with bands 1–13. Instead of band 14, stretch the original orange topper band, which now has your first petal attached to it, over the peg in its place. Ensure the loom is facing the right way.

7. Repeat steps 1–6 five times more, until you have six petals in total all attached to the single orange topper band.

8. Lay the loom for a single chain, as in project 1, with your 24 green bands. Turn the loom so the arrow is facing down towards you and stretch your orange topper band over the first left-hand peg.

9. Put your hook in the first left-hand peg, loop the green band diagonally to the upper right-hand peg. Continue looping the green bands in a zig-zag pattern to the end of the loom.

10. Attach the two ends of the last band with a C-clip, pull off the loom, and attach the C-clip onto the orange topper band.

20. FLOWER GARLAND

Loom configuration: SQUARED

You will need (for six flowers)

6 orange

48 pink

59 green

1 C-clip

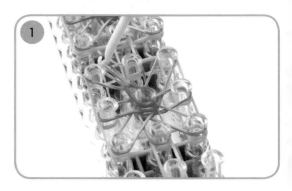

Place the loom with the arrows facing away from you and lay the bands as per the diagram.

1. Turn the loom so the arrow is facing down towards you. Put your hook through the peg in the centre of the bottom square shape. Push the topper band with the back of your hook and catch the first band, looping it back to its original peg on the upper left-hand side.

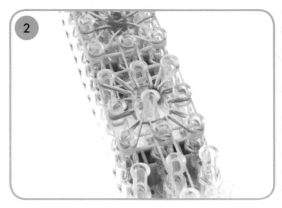

2. Repeat this process for the remaining seven bands, working in a anticlockwise direction. The topper band should now be evenly stretched around the central peg.

3. Repeat this process with the other two square shapes on the loom.

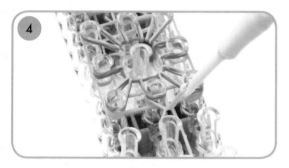

4. Put your hook through the second peg up in the central row, hook the bottom band, and loop it forward.

5. Placing your hook through the peg you just ended on, take the second-to-bottom band and loop it to its original peg on the left-hand side.

6. Repeat this looping three times up the left-hand side to end on the middle top peg of the square.

7. Repeat steps 4 and 5 to the right-hand side, to meet the other bands at the middle top peg of the square.

8. Put your hook back through the middle top peg, catch the bottom band, and loop it forward.

9. Repeat looping the green bands, using steps 5–8 for the remaining two squares, to the end of the loom.

10. Put your hook securely through the two ends of the band looped on the last peg and pull off the loom. Put to one side.

11. Lay the loom for a second time to repeat, except this time, don't lay band 57, and, in the place of band 47, stretch the two ends of the band currently looped on your hook over the pegs instead.

12. Repeat steps 1–9. Finally, put your hook through the last peg, use a C-clip on the two ends, and attach to the other end of the bracelet to complete.

CHAPTER 2
RINGS WITH BLING

Rings are a really fun and quick project to work on, and generally don't use too many bands. There are loads of cool designs to experiment with, and it's easy to personalise them. By simply choosing a unique bead or button, you can create incredibly eye-catching jewellery that will impress all your friends. All the designs here can be easily adapted to suit your finger size by adding extra bands in the chain, before looping. Alternatively, you can extend them on your hook by threading new band links as shown in the Introduction on page 8.

21. CELTIC

Loom configuration: STAGGERED

You will need

10 black
2 green
1 bead
1 C-clip

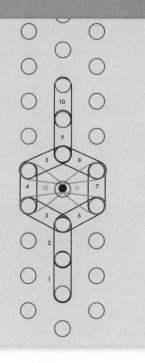

Place the loom with the arrows facing away from you and lay the bands as per the diagram. When placing the green bands, thread them both through the centre of the bead, before stretching between the pegs.

1.Turn the loom so the arrow is facing down toward you. Put your hook through the second central peg, take the bottom band, and loop it forwards.

2. Putting your hook through the third peg, hook the second-to-bottom band, and loop it to its original peg on the upper left-hand side.

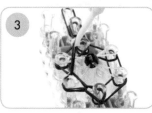

3. Put your hook inside the peg you just finished on, and take the bottom band forward to its original peg, keeping the green band in place.

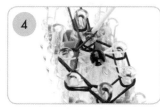

4. Repeat with the next band, taking it from the inside of the peg to its original peg in the central row. Repeat for the three other bands on the right-hand side.

5. Put your hook through the central peg you just finished on, and take the bottom band from the inside and loop forward.

6. Repeat with the next band in the chain. Attach the two band ends with a C-clip, pull off the loom, and join the other end of the ring into the C-clip, too.

22. SPOT FLOWER

Loom configuration: STAGGERED

You will need

11 tie-dye pink
4 white
1 C-clip

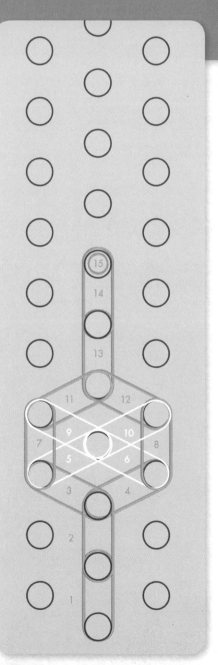

Place the loom with the arrows facing away from you and lay the bands as per the diagram. Don't forget topper band 15!

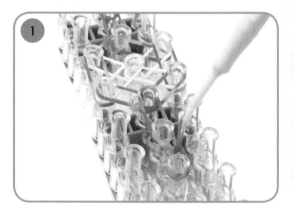

1. Turn the loom so the arrow is facing down towards you. Put your hook through the first central peg, push back the topper band, and loop the bottom band forward. Make sure the topper band doesn't pop off!

2. Put your hook through the second peg, hook the bottom band, and loop it forward.

3. Put your hook inside the third peg, hook the second-to-bottom band, and loop it to its original peg on the upper left-hand side.

7. Put your hook inside the central peg and loop the second band from the bottom to its original peg on the upper left-hand side.

4. At the peg you just finished on, hook the second band from the bottom (shown in white), and loop it to its original peg in the centre.

8. Putting your hook inside the peg you just finished on, take the bottom band, and loop it to the upper central peg.

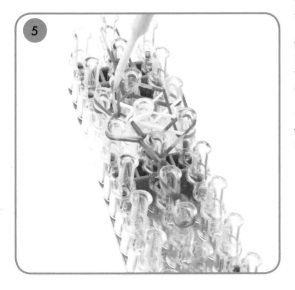

9. Repeat steps 7 and 8 on the right-hand side. **10.** Put your hook inside the peg you just finished on, take the bottom band, and loop it forward to its original peg.

11. Repeat step 10 for the remaining band. Secure with a C-clip, pull the ring off the loom, and attach it to the other end of the ring to complete.

5. Go back inside the first peg used on the left, hook the bottom band, and loop it forward.

6. Repeat steps 3–5 on the right-hand side.

23. BOW

Loom configuration: SQUARED

You will need
4 black
8 white
16 pink
1 C-clip

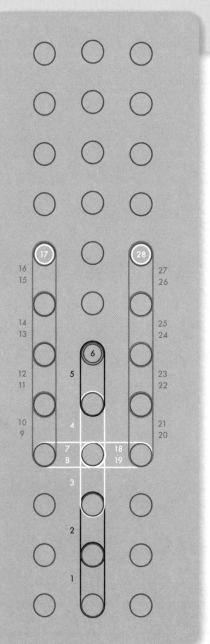

Place the loom with the arrows facing away from you and lay the bands as per the diagram. Bands 7–16 and 18–27 are applied in pairs. Don't forget topper bands 6, 17, and 28!

1. Turn the loom so the arrow is facing down towards you. Put your hook inside the first peg on the left-hand side with a band on, push back the topper band, and loop the bottom pair of bands forward to the next peg.

2. Repeat this looping for the next three pairs of bands of the same colour. When you get to what would be the fourth, hook the pair of bands from the inside and loop them to their original peg, which is to the right-hand side, in the central row.

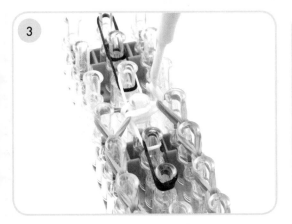

3. Repeat steps 1 and 2 from the first peg on the right-hand side. Make sure you push the bands down well on the central peg.

4. Keeping one finger on the central peg you just finished on to ensure no bands pop off, pull the links you just looped part way off the loom, leaving the end attached to the central peg.

5. Loop the other end (which had the topper band on it) onto the central peg underneath your finger.

6. Put your hook inside the first used peg in the central row. Push back the topper band and link the bottom band forward to its original peg.

7. Repeat this for the four remaining bands, looping each one forward and taking extra care around the busiest peg to ensure you only catch the very bottom band.

8. Once you make it to the end of the loom, join the two band ends with a C-clip, pull the whole thing off the loom, and attach both ends together to complete your ring.

24. RAINBOW HEART

Loom configuration: 2 LOOMS, STAGGERED

You will need

41 assorted colours (all shown red in diagram)

1 C-clip

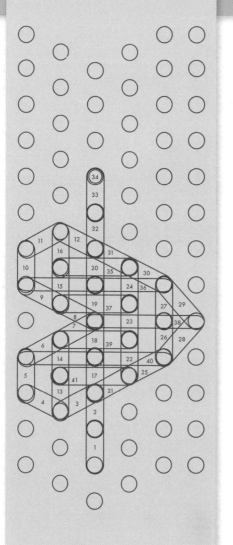

Start by making sure that your loom configuration matches the one in the diagram. Rows 1–5 are staggered, but row 6 is squared with the 5. Now turn the loom so that the arrow is facing away from you. Loop bands 1–41 as pictured in the layout. Please note that band 34 is a topper band and that bands 36–41 are horizontal bands, stretching across multiple pegs.

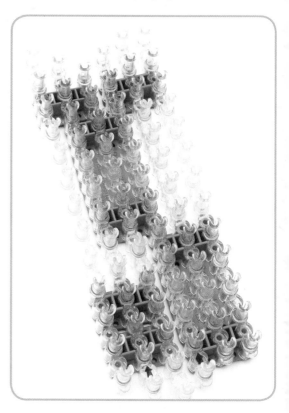

3. Whenever you come to a horizontal band, insert the hook into the peg to push it back before hooking the band beneath it. The horizontal bands remain in the same position the entire time.

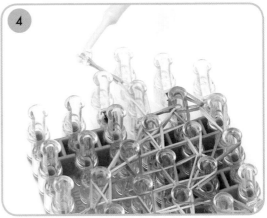

1. Turn the loom around so the arrow is facing you. Beginning at the bottom central peg, start looming the bands in the reverse order that you laid them in. Insert the hook into the peg to push the topper band back, and hook on to the band beneath.

4. When you have reached the last peg, hook all of the bands on it with a C-clip.

5. Remove your project from the loom and hook the C-clip to the topper band to close the ring.

2. Pull up and off the hook, stretching the band back to the peg it started from. Continue on to the next bands and make sure that you are following the correct order down the left side, the four central rows, then the right side. If you have trouble remembering the correct reverse order, refer to the diagram.

25. DAHLIA

Loom configuration: **SQUARED**

You will need

14 orange
8 pink
1 blue
1 C-clip

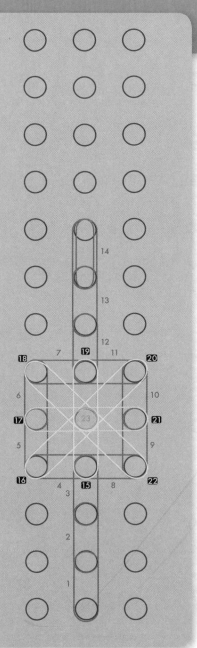

Place the loom with the arrows facing away from you and lay the bands as per the diagram. Wrap band 14 and blue topper twice between the pegs.

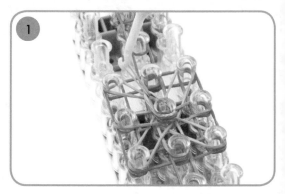

1. Turn the loom so the arrow is facing down toward you. Put your hook through the peg that is central to the square shape. Push the topper band with the back of your hook, catch the first band, and loop it back to its original peg on the upper left-hand side.

2. Repeat this process for the seven remaining bands, working in an anticlockwise direction. The topper band should now be evenly stretched around the central peg.

3. Put your hook through the centre of the second peg up in the chain and loop this band forward. Repeat with the next band up.

4. Placing your hook through the peg you just ended on, take the second-to-bottom band, and loop it to its original peg on the left-hand side.

5. Repeat this looping three times up the left-hand side to end on the middle top peg of the square.

6. Repeat steps 4 and 5 on the right-hand side to meet the other bands at the middle top peg of the square.

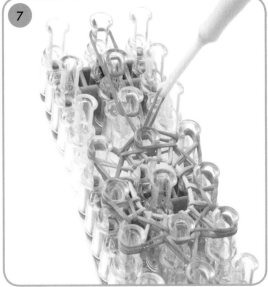

7. Put your hook back through the middle top peg, catch the bottom band, and loop it forward. Repeat this twice more, until you get to the end peg.

8. Attach the band ends with a C-clip, pull off the loom, and fasten to the other end to complete your ring.

J4F!

Why not try blinging up your ring by adding a bead to bands 15–22? Simply slide the band through the centre of the bead before positioning it on the loom. This is sure to make you stand out from the crowd!

26. BEJEWELLED

Loom configuration: STAGGERED

You will need

15 clear yellow
19 shiny green
1 C-clip

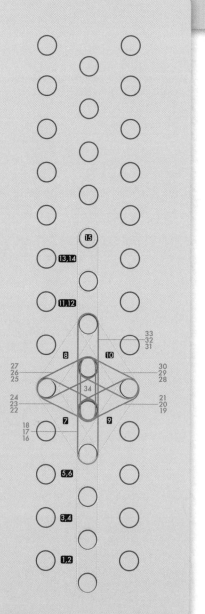

Place the loom with the arrows facing away from you and lay the bands as per the diagram. Don't forget topper band 15! Band 34 is doubled over between the two pegs.

1. Turn the loom so the arrow is facing down toward you. Put your hook inside the fourth central peg up, push back doubled band 34, and take the top trio of bands towards you, back to their original peg. This will be the third peg in the central row.

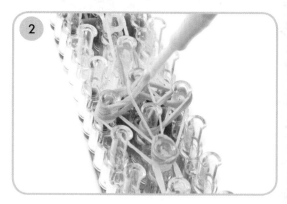

2. Put your hook back in the fourth central peg, push back the topper band, get the next trio of bands, and take to their original peg on the upper left-hand side.

3. Repeat step 2 for the last trio of bands on the upper right-hand side.

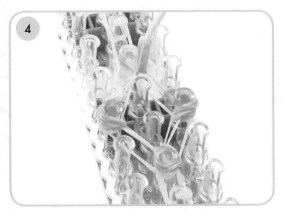

4. Move your hook to the fifth central peg and repeat steps 1–3.

5. Put your hook inside the first central peg, push back topper band 15, and hook the pair of bands forward. Repeat with the next pair of bands.

6. Now put your hook inside the third central peg, take the second-to-bottom band, and loop it to its original peg on the upper left-hand side. Loop the next yellow band forward to its original peg on the upper right-hand side in the central row.

7. Repeat step 6 for the right-hand side.

8. Put your hook in the sixth central peg, carefully reach down to the bottom pair of bands, and loop them forward to the next peg along.

9. Continue to loop forward the remaining pair of bands in the chain. Join both ends of the band with a C-clip, pull off the loom, and attach to the other end to complete the ring.

27. CHEVRON

Loom configuration: ONLY REQUIRES 2 PEGS

You will need

10 black
10 white
2 'spare' bands
1 C-clip

With this fishtail design you'll be hooking from the outside of the pegs. Choose two pegs that are side-by-side to start on.

1. Take your first rubber band, hook it over the first peg, twist it once, and put it onto the adjacent peg to make a figure 8.

2. Without twisting, put a contrasting band around the two pegs. Then, without twisting, place another band in the same colour as the original band, on top of these.

3. Hook the bottom band from the right-hand side of the twist over the right-hand peg. Repeat with the left-hand side of the twist over the left peg. The bottom band is now off the pegs, suspended around the two remaining bands.

4. Stretch another contrasting band between the two pegs and above the others.

5. Repeat step 3, looping the bottom band first off the right-hand peg and then over the left, to suspend it over the remaining bands.

6. Add another contrasting band, and loop the bottom band up off the pegs and over it. Keep doing this with the remaining bands, using your two spare bands last.

7. Put your C-clip around the ends of the last looped band, bring up the bottom end of the ring, and link through the clip, too.

8. Take the ring off the loom and pull out the two spare bands.

28. STAR

Loom configuration: STAGGERED

You will need

12 yellow
5 light blue
1 C-clip

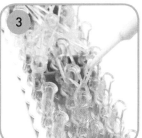

2. Repeat this for the four remaining arms of the star. Make sure you always take from inside the topper bands, and take care as they will be quite tight. When you've done all five, it will look like this.

3. Now, working from the first central peg, put your hook inside, push back topper band 7, hook the bottom band, and loop it forward.

4. Repeat this five more times to the end of the loom. Take extra care at the central peg, as there are a lot of bands. It is important that you only loop the bottom band, and be gentle to avoid it snapping.

5. Once you get to the end of the loom, slide the two ends of the last band into a C-clip, ease your ring off the loom, and attach to the other end to complete it.

Place the loom with the arrows facing away from you and lay the bands as per the diagram. Don't forget topper band 7. Topper bands 13–17 are wrapped four times around the peg to make them nice and tight!

1. Turn the loom so the arrow is facing down towards you. Loop each of the star's arms back to the centre point by hooking through the topper band.

29. KNUCKLEDUSTER

Loom configuration:
SQUARED, MIDDLE ROW REMOVED

You will need

60 red (split into 4 piles of 15)
16 white
4 pink
4 beads of your choice
1 C-clip

Place the loom with the arrows facing away from you and lay the bands as per the diagram. You are going to have to re-lay the left-hand column three more times in this way with the remaining red bands. Don't forget topper bands!

1. Turn the loom so the arrow is facing down towards you. You are only going to be looping the bands on the right-hand row for now (shown in red). Put your hook inside the first peg in the chain, push back topper band 15, and hook the bottom band forward through it.

2. Keep looping to the end of the loom. Now, put your hook through the two ends of the last band and pull off the loom.

3. Stretch the two band ends off your hook and over the second peg in the left-hand row.

4. Re-lay your loom with another set of red bands, as per the diagram. Remember to check the arrow direction before laying the bands! Loop them in the same way as steps 1 and 2. Once you've pulled the design off the loom with the two band ends on the hook, stretch them over the fourth peg on the left-hand row.

7. At the unattached end of each red chain, you will see the doubled-over topper band. Put both loops of the topper band over the peg with a beaded band on. These pegs will have quite a few bands on now, so you may need to push them down.

8. Repeat step 7 with the three remaining red chains.

5. Repeat steps 1 and 2, twice more. Place the next chain on the sixth peg and the chain after on the eighth peg of the left-hand row.

9. Put your hook inside the first peg on the left-hand row, push back the topper band, hook the bottom pair of bands, and loop forward.

10. Loop the remaining six pairs of white bands forward in this way. Make sure to catch only those in your hook and always hook from inside the pegs.

11. Put your hook through the last peg, catch your last white finishing band, and pull one end up and through into a slipknot to finish.

6. Thread a pink band through each of the four beads. Carefully loop both ends of one band over the second peg. Repeat on the fourth, sixth, and eighth pegs.

12. To tidy up, wrap the end of the slipknot band a few times around the closest bead. On the other end, you can stretch the doubled topper band over the closest band for a really cool finish!

30. CUTE AS A BUTTON

Loom configuration: STAGGERED

You will need

13 green
1 button
1 C-clip

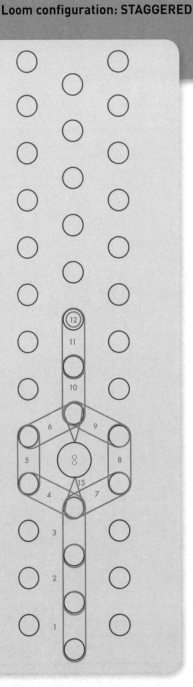

Place the loom with the arrows facing away from you, and lay the bands as per the diagram. To attach the button band, thread a single band through the two holes and stretch between the two pegs.

1. Turn the loom so the arrow is facing down towards you. Put your hook inside the first central peg, push back the topper band, catch the bottom band, and loop it forward.

2. Loop forward the next band in the same way.

3. Put your hook inside the third peg, taking the band second from the bottom, and loop it to its original peg on the upper left-hand side. Make sure you take it from inside the other bands on the peg.

6. Putting your hook inside the central peg you just ended on, take the bottom band, looping it up through all the other bands, onto the peg in front.

7. Loop the next two bands in the chain forward in the same way.

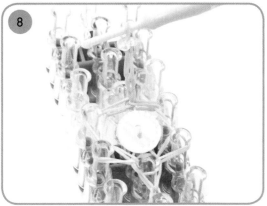

4. Loop forward the next two bands in the chain in the same way, back to their original pegs. With the second one, its original peg is in the central row.

5. Repeat steps 3 and 4 on the right-hand side, but this time start by looping the very bottom band from inside the third peg.

8. Attach the two ends of the last band with a C-clip. Pull the ring off the loom, and slip the other end of it into a C-clip to finish.

OMG!

The great thing about this ring is that it is so easily altered by the type of button you use. So why not make a full collection?

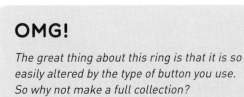

CHAPTER 3
FUNKY ACCESSORIES

No outfit is complete without accessories! There's so much more you can do with bands than you might first imagine, and we'll explore some of those ideas through the projects in this chapter. There's a mixture of practical and fun designs that will really test your looming skills, as well as being useful in day-to-day life. Some of these are easily adaptable, so don't be afraid to push yourself and develop them further. There are some really cool costume pieces, too, which are ideal from prom to Halloween!

31. HOOPLA EARRINGS

Loom configuration: STAGGERED

You will need

8 yellow	8 green
8 orange	2 white
8 red	2 black (to be
8 purple	cut off)
8 blue	2 earring hooks

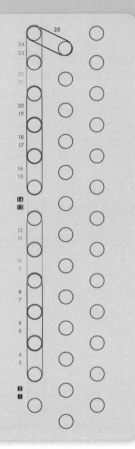

Place the loom with the arrows facing away from you and lay the bands as per the diagram. Bands 1–24 are applied to the loom in pairs. You will re-lay the loom with the remaining bands to make the second earring.

1

1. Turn the loom so the arrow is facing down towards you. Put your hook inside the first peg on the right-hand side and loop the bottom pair of bands forward. Keep the black band in place.

2. Put your hook in the second peg, catch the bottom pair of bands, and loop them forward.

3. Keep looping forward like this to the end of the loom.

4

4. Put your hook through the last pair of band ends and pull the whole thing off the loom.

5

5. Follow the black band through the ends it goes through, and slide them onto your hook.

6

6. Carefully cut off the black band. Take a white band on the end of your hook and pull through the band ends on your hook.

7

7. Loop the other end of the white band onto the hook, so the earring is suspended from the hook by the white band.

8

8. Slide these two white ends into your earring hook link, and close with pliers if necessary.

9. Re-lay the loom and repeat steps 1–8 to make the second earring and complete your snazzy pair.

32. BOW TIE

Loom configuration:
SQUARED AND MINI LOOM

You will need
202 black
15 white
1 C-clip

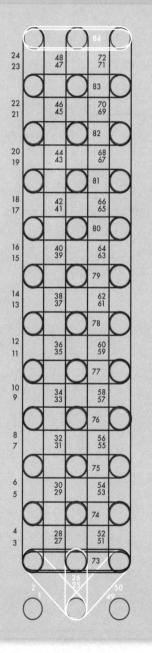

Place the loom with the arrows facing away from you, and lay the bands as per the diagram. You will have to lay the loom like this twice to complete this bow, and a third time to complete a neck chain.

1. Turn the loom so the arrow is facing down towards you. Put your hook in the first peg on the left-hand side, push back the topper band, hook the bottom pair of bands, and loop forward.

2. Continue looping the pairs of bands like this to the end of the loom. Make sure each time that you hook from the inside of the peg, and pull the bottom pair of bands up through the centre of the other bands before looping forward.

3. When you get to the last pair of bands in the chain, loop in the same style, to the last central peg of the loom, the bands' original peg.

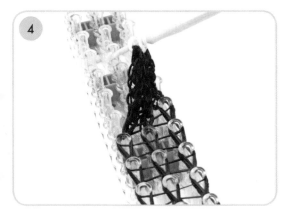

7. Put your hook through all the bands on the last central peg, and pull off the loom. Loop the topper band from the side of the bow you just created onto your hook as well.

4. Repeat steps 1–3 for the central row, and then the right-hand row. Put your hook through all the bands on the last central peg, and, making sure they stay on the hook, pull the rest of the bands off the loom. Put this to one side and re-lay your loom as in the original diagram, remembering to have the arrows pointing away from you when you do so.

8. Hook a white band onto the end of your hook, being super careful not to lose any bands, slide it through them all, then through itself to create a slipknot.

5. Once you've placed all the bands, with the arrows still facing away from you, carefully stretch the bands off your hook and over the first central peg.

9. Stretch the white slipknot over the Mini Loom (see page 9) and extend each side by 24 black bands before attaching both ends together with a C-clip.

6. Get the topper band from the other end of the bow and loop it onto the same first central peg. Repeat steps 1–4.

33. PENCIL GRIP

Loom configuration: SQUARED

You will need

44 pink

44 yellow

44 turquoise

1 pencil or

pen

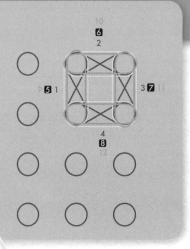

Place the loom with the arrows facing toward you. Remove the blue connector directly below the pegs you will be working on and lay the first twelve bands as per the diagram.

1. At the first central peg, hook the bottom two bands (that are the same colour) from the outside and loop over the top of the peg.

2. Do the same for the second peg, and then again for the two remaining pegs in a clockwise direction. Once you've looped all four pegs, it will look like this.

FTW!

This is enough to make a standard pencil grip, but, if you'd prefer it longer, simply add more bands!

3. Push the bands down the pegs. Now add another layer of four bands, the same colour as the ones you just looped. Lay them in a clockwise direction, always starting from the first central peg.

4. Now repeat steps 1–3 ten times, or until your pencil grip is as long as you want it. Keep pushing it down.

5. Hook over the bottom two bands once more, in a clockwise direction, leaving you with just two bands on each peg.

6. Put your hook inside the first central peg, and slide both bands securely onto the wide part of your hook.

7. Repeat this in a clockwise direction for the remaining three pegs. Your pencil grip will come off the loom and hold on your hook.

8. Take your pencil and gently slide it into the pencil grip, making sure the band ends stay on the hook.

9. Once the pencil pokes out of the top, stretch the two sets of bands nearest the end of your hook over the point of your pencil and off the hook.

10. Finish the holder off by stretching the remaining two sets of bands over the pencil and off the hook, in the same way as step 9.

34. HOT DRINKS HOLDER

Loom configuration:
2 LOOMS SQUARED, ATTACHED SIDEWAYS

You will need

12 black
138 white
138 red
72 yellow

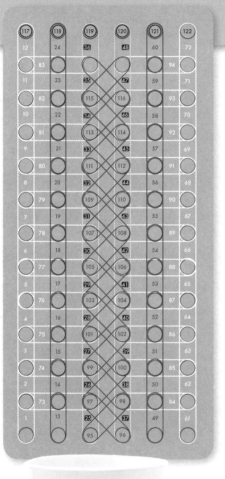

Place the loom with the arrows facing away from you, and lay the bands as per the diagram. You will have to lay the loom like this three times to complete the pattern.

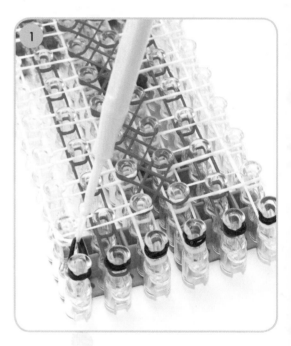

1

1. Turn the loom so the arrow is facing down toward you. Place your hook down through the first left-hand peg, hook the bottom band, and loop forward to the peg in front.

2. Put your hook through the second left-hand peg, hook the bottom band, and loop forward to its original peg in front. Continue to loop the left-hand side up to the end on the loom. Each time make sure that you are putting your hook through the inside of the peg to collect the bands, rather than the outside!

3. Repeat the process with the remaining five rows of pegs.

4. Put your hook through the last peg on the left-hand side, and slide the bands off the peg and onto the wide part of your hook.

5. Repeat this with the five other pegs, from left to right. Once the bands from all six pegs are on the hook, pull the rest off the loom. Put to one side.

6. Turn the loom so the arrows are facing away from you, and re-lay the loom with bands 1–116. Instead of adding topper bands 117–122, you are going to stretch the band ends off your hook to their corresponding colored peg, from right to left.

7 . Repeat steps 1–6, to lengthen your piece, and then repeat steps 1–5 to get it to its complete length.

8. With the loom arrows facing away from you, lay five black bands on the left-hand row. Instead of adding topper bands, starting at the furthest peg, stretch the bands' ends off your hook, and put a pair on each of the six pegs.

9. Fold your drinks holder, so that six black topper bands match up with the six pegs. Stretch both loops of them over their corresponding pegs.

10. Turn your loom so the arrows are facing towards you, put your hook inside the first peg, hook the bottom band, and loop forward.

11 . Carry on looping the bottom black bands forward to the end of the chain, and finish off by using your last black band to create a slipknot through the last peg. Pull off the loom and slide onto your cup!

FYI!

BE CAREFUL! Always slide onto your cup before filling with a hot drink to avoid spillage!

35. SKATER BELT

Loom configuration: 2 LOOMS STAGGERED, ATTACHED LONGWAYS

You will need

56 black
52 white
200 green
2 C-clips

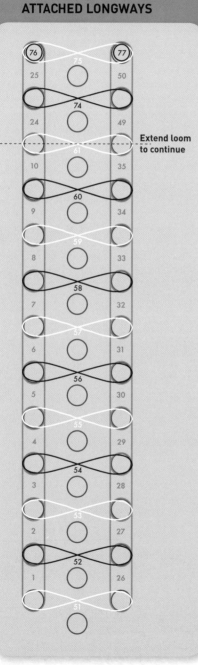

Extend loom to continue

Place the loom with the arrows facing away from you, and lay the bands as per the diagram. You will have to lay the loom like this about four times to complete a 70 cm (28 in.) belt.

1. Turn the loom so the arrow is facing down toward you. Place your hook down through the first left-hand peg, hook the bottom band, and loop forward to the peg in front.

2. Put your hook through the second left-hand peg, hook the bottom band, and loop forward to its original peg in front. Continue to loop the left-hand side up to the end on the loom. Each time, make sure that you are putting your hook through the inside of the peg to collect the bands, rather than the outside!

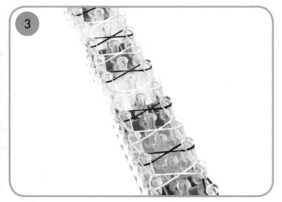

3. Repeat the process on the right-hand row of pegs.

4. Put your hook into the last left-hand peg and slide both the ends of the band onto the wide part of your hook and off the peg.

5. Repeat step 4 on the right-hand side. Now, with both sides securely on the hook, pull the rest of the bands off the loom. Put to one side.

6. Re-lay the loom, but don't lay topper bands 76 and 77. Instead, stretch the first two band ends off your hook and onto one peg, and the second two band ends off your hook onto the other peg.

7. Repeat steps 1–6 at least twice more (depending on how long you'd like the belt) and then finish off by repeating steps 1–3.

8. Now, put your hook in the last left-hand peg, pull a black band through, and create a slipknot. Repeat on the last right-hand peg and pull off the loom. Attach both ends using a C-clip.

BTW!

You will need to repeat steps 1–6 if you want to make the belt longer.

36. BAREFOOT SANDAL

Loom configuration: STAGGERED

You will need

24 white
24 purple
35 turquoise
1 C-clip

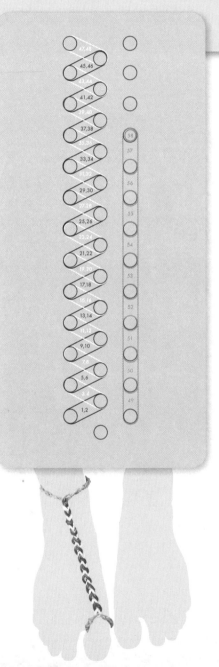

Place the loom with the arrows facing away from you, and lay the bands as per the diagram.

1. Turn the loom so the arrow is facing down towards you. Place your hook down through the first left-hand peg, push back the topper band, hook the bottom band, and loop it forward to the peg in front.

2. Loop the turquoise bands like this until the end of the chain. Put your hook through the last peg of the chain, and slide the two band ends onto it and off the peg. Pull the rest of the chain off the loom.

3. Now, moving to the first right-hand peg, slide the band ends off the hook and onto the peg.

4. Then, hold the other end of the turquoise chain, and stretch both loops of the last band (which was the topper band) over the first right-hand peg, too.

5. Now, let's loop! Put your hook inside the first right-hand peg, push back the turquoise bands, take the bottom two bands, and loop them forward to the upper left-hand side.

6. Moving in a zig-zag pattern up the loom, keep looping the bottom pair of bands back to their original peg, alternately to the upper left and right. Once you get to the end, put your hook through the last peg and slide both band ends onto the wide part of the hook. Pull the rest of the bands off the loom and set side.

7. Now, turn your loom so the arrows face away from you. You are going to re-lay your loom with 24 turquoise bands. Arrange them in the same formation as bands 1–48 on the diagram, but this time just use single bands instead of doubles. Put a topper band on the very last peg in the chain.

8. Turn your loom back around so the arrows point towards you. Count to the seventh peg in the right-hand row, and carefully stretch the bands off your hook and onto the peg.

9. Now put your hook in the first peg on the right-hand side, push back the topper band, take the bottom band, and loop it to its original peg on the upper left-hand side.

10. Continue to hook and loop in a zig-zag pattern to the end of the loom, remembering to always take the bottom band from inside the pegs, and not to loop it around the outside.

11. Once you get to the end of the loom, attach the last two band ends with a C-clip, pull the whole thing off the loom, and slide the other end of the anklet into the clip to complete your barefoot sandal.

FYI!

You can easily adjust the sandal to make it longer or shorter by simply using more or fewer bands in your chains.

37. TIARA

Loom configuration: **STAGGERED**

You will need

6 white
24 purple
78 pink
1 hair band

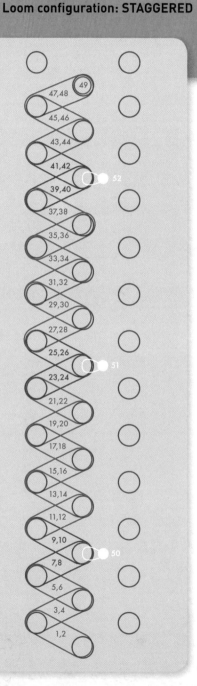

Place the loom with the arrows facing away from you, and lay the bands as per the diagram. You will have to lay it like this twice to make a six-peak tiara.

1. Turn the loom so the arrow is facing down towards you. Place your hook down through the first central peg, push back the topper band, hook the bottom pair of bands, and take them to their original peg on the upper right-hand side.

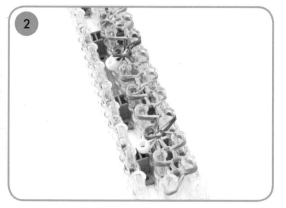

2. Keep looping the rest of the pairs of bands in this way, working in a zig-zag pattern, making sure you always put your hook inside the peg and take the bottom pair of bands through the others.

3. Once you get to the end of the loom, put your hook in the last peg, slide the bands onto it, and pull it off the loom.

4. Take your head band, and slide the two bands off the hook and onto the hair band.

5. Then, find the three topper bands along the chain, and stretch them over the hair band, too.

6. Re-lay the loom with your remaining bands and repeat steps 1–5 to complete your tiara. Make sure the bands are evenly spaced along your band.

IU2U!

Why not try it with some sparkly beads to really glam it up?

38. CAT EARS

Loom configuration: SQUARED

You will need

70 black
16 white
2 spare bands
(to be cut)
1 black hair
band

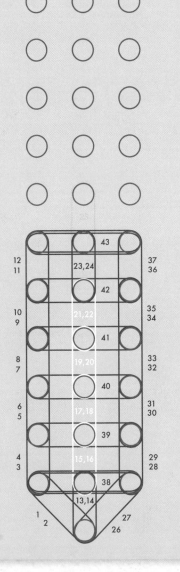

Place the loom with the arrows facing away from you, and lay the bands as per the diagram. Bands 38 and 43 are doubled over the pegs.

1. Turn the loom so the arrow is facing down towards you. Starting on the left-hand side, put your hook through the first left peg, and loop the bottom pair of bands forward, being careful not to let the top band ping off!

2. Carry on looping the remaining five pairs of bands in this row forward, ending on the top central peg.

84

3. Repeat this for the central row, starting at the first pair of black bands, and then again for the right-hand-side row. All rows should come together on the top central peg.

4. Put your hook through the top central peg, and out of the bottom of all the bands, to catch a new black band. Loop this back through itself to create a slipknot.

5. Pull the ear off the loom. This is your first one! Re-load the loom and repeat the process so you have two ears.

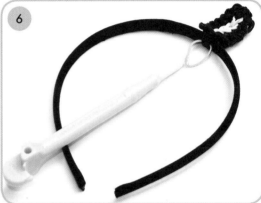

6. Tuck the slipknots at the top of the ears in. At the bottom of the ears, the 'spare' band should be poking out in a loop. Pull it gently so it reveals the bands it loops through. These are the ones that you then need to slide along your hair band.

7. Once you've positioned both ears on the hair band, cut off the 'spare' band that hangs loose and admire your purrr-fect creation!

39. GLASSES SLEEVE

Loom configuration: STAGGERED

You will need

24 green
24 pink
24 purple
1 pair of glasses
or sunglasses

Place the loom with the arrows facing toward you.

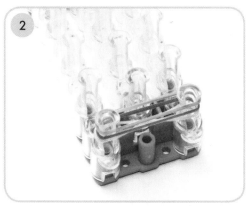

1. Stretch your first band between the first left- and right-hand peg, in a figure of 8.

2. Stretch your second coloured band between the same two pegs, and then the third.

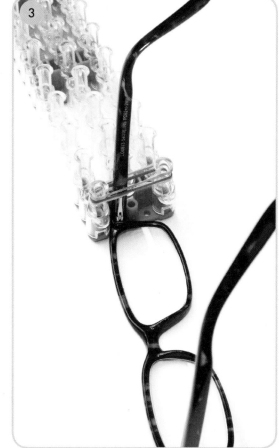

3. Now, put the arm of your glasses up between the three bands, to the left of the cross in the first band.

6. Repeat steps 4 and 5 until you have used 12 bands of each colour, or until you've reached your desired length. Then, take the bottom band over again as you normally would, leaving you with just one band on the pegs. Carefully stretch the band from the left-hand peg over the top of the arm. Then stretch the band from the right-hand peg over the glasses, too.

4. Hook the bottom band from outside the left-hand peg and loop over the peg. Repeat on the right-hand side.

7. Now repeat steps 1–6 for the other arm of your glasses.

FYEO!

Your glasses will never rub your ears again, and they will look really personalised too. Put a cloth down to prevent you from scratching your glasses.

5. Take a band the same colour as the one you just looped, and stretch it down over the arm of your glasses and between the two pegs.

40. PEARL NECKLACE

Loom configuration: 2 LOOMS ATTACHED LONGWAYS, STAGGERED

You will need

49 gold
24 white
24 pearly beads
1 O-clip

Extend loom
to continue

Place the loom with the arrows facing away from you; lay the bands and strung beads as per diagram.

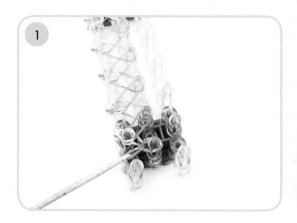

1. Turn the loom so the arrow is facing down towards you. Place your hook through the first central peg and loop the bottom band to its original peg, on the upper left-hand side.

2. Put your hook through the peg you just finished and loop the bottom band to its original peg on the upper right-hand side.

88

3

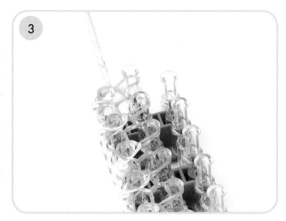

3. Repeat this process to the end of the loom.

4

4. Put your hook through the final peg and attach the two ends of the last band with an O-clip.

5

5. Pull off the loom and link the other end of the necklace into the O-clip.

FTW!

Why not make an elegant set with a pearly bracelet to match!

CHAPTER 4
LUCKY CHARMS

Charms are adaptable and can be used in many ways. There's a mix of simple and more complex designs here to challenge you. Some will require more patience than others! However, once you master them, they are definitely worth the effort and very satisfying to make. They're ideal for gifts and make cute decorations around the home. You can easily attach them to your keys, use them on rings, and loop them into bracelets or hair clips. For something slightly different, why not try turning one into a brooch for an instant wearable charm!

41. UNICORN

Loom configuration: SQUARED

You will need

58 white   3 green
4 pink   3 yellow
4 blue   1 gold
7 purple

DIAGRAM 1   **DIAGRAM 2**

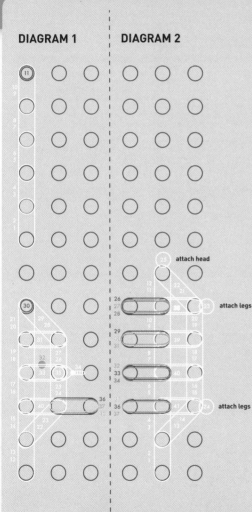

attach head

attach legs

attach legs

Place the loom with the arrows facing away from you and lay the bands as per diagram 1. Topper bands 11 and 30 are wrapped four times around the pegs.

EYES

For bands 32 and 33, wrap blue band 32 four times around the hook, stretch white band 33 from the end of your hook and slide the blue band onto it. Put both ends of the white band onto your hook, and stretch them both between the pegs as shown. This will become the eyes.

HORN

Band 34 is your unicorn horn! Take a single gold band, twist it a few times, and tie a knot at one end of it. Stretch the small end over the peg.

EARS

Band 35 is a topper band that has gone twice around the peg and will become the ears.

1. Turn the loom so the arrow is facing down toward you. We're going to start with the legs. Put your hook in the first right-hand peg, push back the topper band, hook the top pair of bands underneath it, and loop them forward to their original peg.

2. Continue looping the four remaining bands in this chain. Put your hook through the last peg in the chain, slide the bands on to it and off the loom.

3. Pull the charm off the loom. You can store it on the first left-hand peg by stretching the bands off your hook and onto the peg. Re-lay the loom with bands 1–11 three more times, each time storing them on the second, third, and fourth left-hand pegs.

4. Now it's time to loop the head. Make sure the arrow is still facing down towards you; put your hook in the eighth peg up (pink topper band 30). Push back the topper band, hook the first pair of white bands, and loop to the upper left-hand side.

5. Put your hook in the peg you just finished on; take the bottom pair of bands and loop forward. Repeat this looping twice more, making sure that both times you put your hook inside the peg and all the bands on it to collect the bottom bands. The last band in this chain will be looped on a diagonal, to the upper right-hand side.

6. Now go back to the eighth peg up (pink topper band 30). Put your hook in, push back the topper band, hook the bottom pair of white bands and loop them forward.

7. Repeat looping this chain in this way for the remaining four bands to the end of the loom. Make sure you always loop from inside the topper bands! Put your hook through the last peg, slide the bands onto it and off the loom, then pull the whole head off the loom. Store it on the first right-hand peg by sliding your bands off the hook and onto that peg.

8. Place the loom with the arrows facing away from you; lay the bands as per diagram 2 on page 91.

9. Turn your loom so the arrow is pointing towards you. First start moving your legs to their pegs. To do this, slide one of them onto your hook, and stretch it over the peg marked on diagram 2 with '23'. Repeat with the second leg on the same peg.

10. Repeat with the other two legs onto the peg marked '24'.

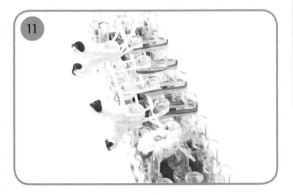

11. Now move the head off the storage peg in the same way, and stretch it onto the peg marked on diagram 2 with '25'. Make sure it's not on upside down. The 'mane' on the head should be on the same side as the 'mane' on the body.

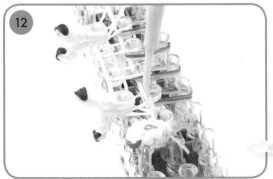

12. You can now start looping the body. Put your hook through the peg you just put your head onto, take the second to bottom pair of bands and loop them to the upper left-hand side.

13. Loop the remaining five bands in this row in the same way, making sure you reach inside the topper bands to hook the bottom bands. The last band in this row will be looped on a diagonal back to the central row.

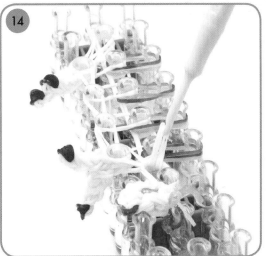

14. Now, go back to the peg that you placed the head on, put your hook inside, and take the very bottom pair of bands. Loop them forward to the peg in front.

15. Repeat this looping for the next five bands in the row. Make sure it's only through the bottom pair of bands that you loop forward. Once you get to the end, pull the bottom band on the last peg up through to create a slipknot. Gently pull your unicorn off the loom.

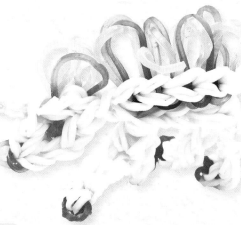

42. BUG

Loom configuration: 2 LOOMS, STAGGERED

You will need

49 purple

6 black

2 black beads

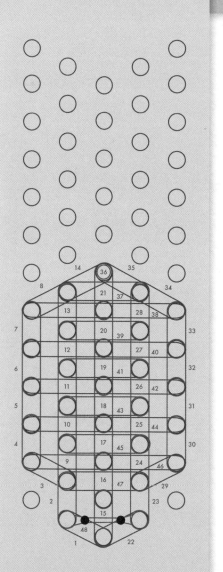

Turn the loom so that the arrow is facing away from you. String the 2 beads across a band. Lay bands 1–36 according to the layout. Band number 36 will be a topper band and bands 37–48 are horizontal bands, stretched across multiple rows. After you string band 48, push the beads to opposite sides of the band. When you finish laying out the bands there will be one purple band and six black bands. These will be used later.

1. Turn the loom around so the arrow is facing you. Begin at band 36. Insert the hook into the peg to push back the topper band. Hook the band beneath and loop it forward to the peg it originated from.

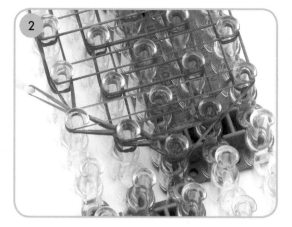

2. Continue looping the bands in the reverse order that you laid them out. Whenever you come to a horizontal band, insert the hook into the peg to pull it back before hooking the band beneath. The horizontal bands will remain in the same place the entire time.

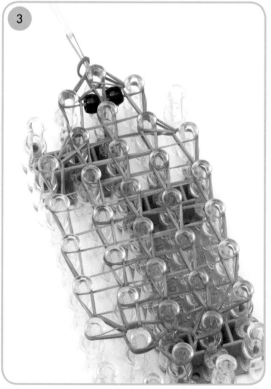

4. Before removing the charm, make slipknots over the loops at the bottom right and left corners. Tighten and then tie the ends into knots, so they'll look more like feet. Repeat at the bug's mid section and the top left and right sides. Remove the charm from the loom.

3. When you get to the last peg, use the hook to insert the purple band through it. Tighten it around the bands on that hook with a slipknot.

43. CUPCAKE

Loom configuration: SQUARED

You will need

2 pink

12 sparkly orange

13 white

1 pink or red bead

Place the loom with the arrows facing away from you, and lay the bands as per the diagram. In this design you'll need to wrap bands 24 and 27 twice around those pegs. To get your bead in position, poke a pink band through it, then stretch both ends of the band over the peg.

1. Turn the loom so the arrow is facing down towards you. Put your hook inside the first left-hand peg, hook the bottom band, and loop it forward to the next peg.

2. Do this three more times in this row, but this time hooking the bottom pair of bands. The last pair of bands should loop to the upper central peg, on the upper right-hand side. Always remember to put your hook inside the peg to get the bottom bands.

4. Put your hook inside this central peg, take the very bottom band (here it's pink), and loop it forward to the top central peg. It will probably be quite tight, so go easy!

5. Finally, from the inside of this peg, hook the bottom of the band through the top of the band to create a slipknot. Gently pull your sweet little cupcake off the loom.

3. Repeat this for the middle row, then the right-hand row, which both will end on the same central peg, one down from the top.

44. STRAWBERRY

Loom configuration: STAGGERED

You will need
19 red
7 green
2 yellow

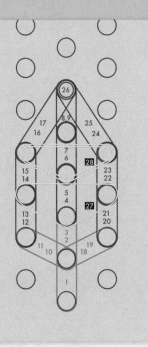

Place the loom with the arrows facing away from you, and lay the bands as per the diagram. Topper band 26 is wrapped around the peg four times, topper band 28 twice, and topper band 27 just once.

1. Turn the loom so the arrow is facing down toward you. Put your hook in the first central peg. Push back the topper band, hook the top pair of bands, and loop diagonally to the upper left-hand side.

2. Continue to loop the next three pairs of bands in the row forward, always going inside the topper band to loop them. The last pair will be looped diagonally to the upper central peg.

3. Put your hook back in the first central peg, and repeat steps 1 and 2 for the right-hand side.

4. Put your hook once more in the first central peg, loop the bottom pair of bands forward. Then loop the next three pairs forward too.

5. Put your hook in the peg you just finished on, reach down, catch the bottom green band, and loop it forward.

6. Loop the bottom end of the band up through the middle of itself, pulling it into a slipknot. Pull your sweet little strawberry off the loom.

45. BUMBLEBEE

Loom configuration: SQUARED

You will need

11 black

8 yellow

26 clear glittery blue

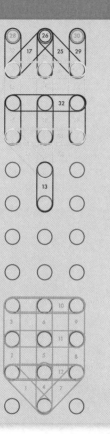

Place the loom with the arrows facing away from you and lay the bands as per the diagram. You are going to need to lay bands 1–12 twice for the wings.

1. Turn the loom so the arrow faces you. Put your hook in the fourth peg down on the left, push back the topper band, and loop the bottom band forward.

2. Repeat step 1 twice more in the row, returning the bands to their original peg. Repeat steps 1 and 2 for the central and right-hand rows. Now put your hook in the last central peg, slide all the bands onto your hook, and pull your wing off the loom.

3. Moving to the third peg up from the bottom on the left-hand side, slide and stretch the bands off your hook and onto this peg.

4. Re-lay the loom with bands 1–12 and repeat steps 1–3, stretching this wing on the third peg up from the bottom on the right-hand side.

5. Put your hook in the first peg up on the left, push back the blue topper band, and hook the bottom band forward. Repeat on the right.

6. Put your hook in the first central peg, push back the topper band, take the first band under it, and loop it to its original peg on the left-hand side.

7. Continue looping the remaining three bands on the left-hand side; the last will be on a diagonal.

8. Repeat steps 6 and 7 for the three bands in the central row, and then for the right-hand row.

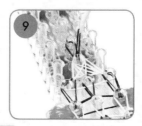

9. Put your hook in the peg that all bands ended on, and hook bottom black band from inside. Loop the bottom through itself into a slipknot. Tie a knot in antenna. Pull off loom.

46. SNAIL

Loom configuration: **SQUARED**, MIDDLE ROW WITH
PEGS FACING OPPOSITE DIRECTION TO THE TWO OUTER ROWS

You will need

12 yellow
50 purple
2 black

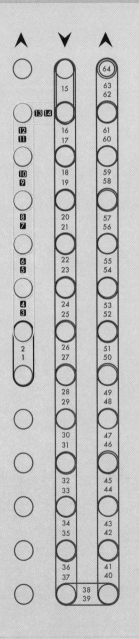

Place the loom with the arrows in the two outer rows facing away from you and the middle row facing towards you. Lay the bands in the order shown on the diagram, making sure to pay extra attention to the numbers. Topper band 64 is wrapped around the peg twice, as is band 15.

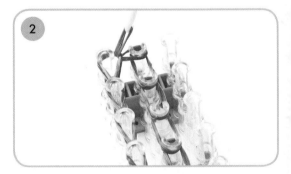

1

1. Turn the loom so the arrows in the outer rows are facing down towards you. Put your hook in the first left-hand peg, push back the topper band, hook the bottom pair of bands, and loop forward.

2

2. Continue looping forward the remaining 11 pairs of bands in this row. Then, putting your hook into the last peg in the row, take the bottom pair of bands and loop to the right-hand side.

3. Turn your loom so the arrows in the middle row are facing toward you. Put your hook in the peg you just finished on (the new first peg in the central row), and take the bottom pairs of bands and loop forward.

4. Continue looping for the next 10 bands in the row. The last band in the chain does not get looped. When you've looped the 10 bands, take the bottom pair of bands and loop to the left-hand side.

7. Pull the whole chain off the loom. Tie a tiny knot in the end of each black band. These are your antennae.

8. Starting at the purple end of the chain, we're now going to create the shell. Take the last band, and then thread the yellow end through it, until it gets tight.

5. Turn your loom so the arrows in the outer rows are facing down towards you. Putting your hook inside the peg you just finished on, loop the next five pairs of bands in the chain forward.

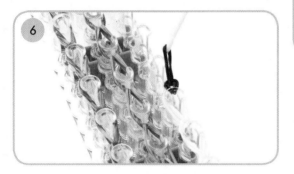

9. Count five bands along from the end, stretch the link out, thread the yellow end through it, and pull tight.

10. Then take the loose purple band where the purple chain turns to yellow and thread it over the yellow end twice.

6. Then, putting your hook in the peg you just finished on, reach down and take the bottom two bands and loop forward. Then pull the bottom ends of them through the inside of the loop you just made to create two slipknots. Pull tight.

OMG!

This one makes a great brooch. Get your brooch pin and thread the back of it through a couple of the bands. It's that simple.

47. BUTTERFLY

Loom configuration: STAGGERED

You will need

32 pink
16 purple
13 black
2 white
4 C-clips

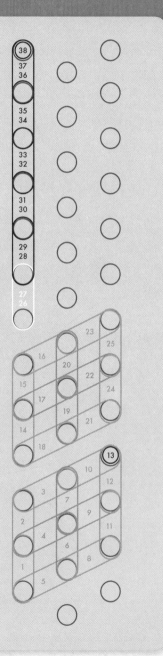

Place the loom with the arrows facing away from you, and lay the bands as shown on the diagram. You'll have to lay bands 1–25 twice. Topper band 13 is wrapped twice around the peg. Topper band 38 is wrapped four times around the peg.

1. Turn the loom so the arrows are facing down toward you. Put your hook in the fourth peg from the top on the left-hand side. Push back the black topper band, take the first pink band, and loop it forward.

2. Put your hook in the peg you just looped to, take the next pink band, and loop forward again; then take the bottom pink band from the peg you just looped to, and loop diagonally to the upper right-hand side.

3. Go back to the third peg from the top on the left-hand side, take the bottom purple band, and loop diagonally to the upper right-hand side, to the peg in the central row.

4. Go to the fourth peg from the top on the left-hand side, push back the topper band, and loop the bottom pink band diagonally to the upper right-hand side.

5. Put your hook in the peg you just finished on, catch the second-to-bottom purple band, and loop forward. Repeat once, being sure to catch only the second-to-bottom purple band.

6. At the peg you just finished on (second from the top in the center), reach down and hook the bottom pink band diagonally to the upper right-hand side.

7. Go back to the central peg third from the top, and loop the bottom purple band to the right-hand side.

8. At the central peg fourth from the top, hook the bottom band and loop to the upper right-hand side. Putting your hook in the peg you just looped to, take the bottom pink band forward. Repeat this once more.

9. Now put your hook through the last peg, and pull your first wing off the loom! Attach the band ends on your hook with a C-clip, and slide off your hook. Stretch the black topper band on the seventh peg from the top on the left-hand side.

10. Repeat the looping pattern from steps 1–10 with this wing, so you finish with two wings attached to one topper band.

11. Re-lay your loom with bands 1–25, making sure the arrows face the right way! Then repeat steps 1–10 to create your second pair of wings.

12. Make sure the loom arrows are facing back towards you. Now we're going to attach the wings to the body. Take your first pair, and stretch the black topper band over the fourth peg up from the bottom on the right-hand side. Then stretch the second pair of wings over the second peg up from the bottom on the right-hand side.

13. Put your hook in the first right-hand peg, push back the topper band and loop the bottom pair of bands forward. Continue looping the next five pairs of bands forward in this way, being careful to always hook from inside the topper bands and only loop the pair you want forward.

14. The last looped pair, the white bands, will become your slipknot. Take the bottom ends of the bands up through the center of the last loop and pull tight.

15. Pull your bands off the loom to see your beautiful butterfly. Finally, tie a little knot in the end of each of the white bands. These are your antennae. You are now ready to fly!

48. OCTOPUS

Loom configuration: SQUARED

You will need

67 orange
2 black
1 blue

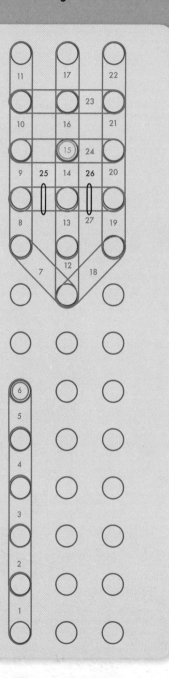

Place the loom with the arrows facing away from you, and lay the bands as per the diagram. You will have to lay bands 1–6 a total of eight times to make the tentacles! Topper bands 6 and 15 must be wrapped around their retrospective pegs four times.

1. To make the eyes band, wrap a black band around your hook four times, and then wrap a second black band around your hook four times. Put an orange band on the end of your hook and pull tight. Slide the black bands onto the orange one and stretch between the pegs, making sure the 'eyes' are evenly spaced.

2. Turn the loom so the arrow is facing down towards you. We're going to start by making the tentacles. Put your hook inside the eighth peg up on the right-hand side. Push back the topper band, hook the bottom band, and loop it forward.

3. Continue looping with the remaining four bands in the chain to the end of the loom. Put your hook through the bands on the last peg and pull the chain off the loom.

4. Stretch the band ends off your hook and onto the first left-hand peg of the loom. This is your first tentacle in place.

5. Re-lay the loom with bands 1–6, and repeat steps 2–4 seven times. You'll want to stretch three tentacles over the first left-hand peg, two tentacles over the first central peg, and three tentacles over the first right-hand peg.

6. Put your hook in the first left-hand peg, hook the bottom band, and loop it forward.

7. Continue hooking the remaining four bands in this chain, making sure you always put your hook inside the topper band. The last band in the chain will be at a diagonal.

8. Repeat steps 5 and 6, for the central and right-hand rows, starting at the first peg. Once the last bands from all three rows are on the top central peg, hook your orange finishing band up through the bands and into a slipknot. Pull off the loom.

FYI!

You can double the bands to create a tighter project, although take care using this technique as bands can snap quite easily.

49. SKATEBOARD

Loom configuration: STAGGERED

You will need

32 white
8 light green
4 black beads

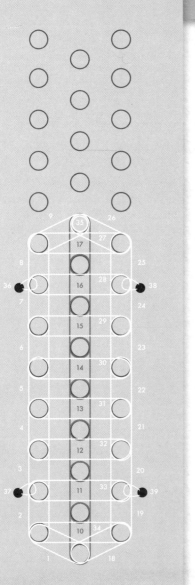

Start by stringing the four black beads onto white bands. Band 35 will be a topper band. Turn the loom so that the arrow is facing away from you. Lay all bands according to the diagram. When you have finished laying out the bands you will have one white band. This will be used as a slipknot at the end.

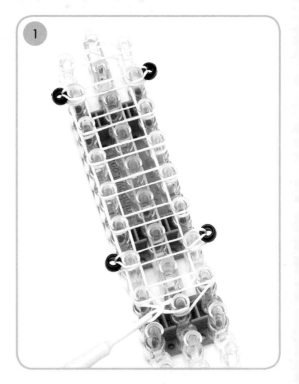

1. Turn the loom around so the arrow is facing you. You will loop the bands in reverse from the order you placed them in. Begin at band 35. Insert the hook into the peg to push back the topper band. Hook the bands beneath and loop forward to the peg they originated from.

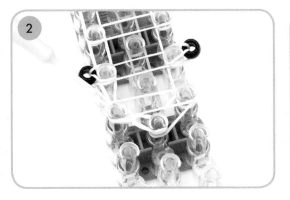

2. On the next band push back the horizontal band before looping the bands beneath it forward. Finish looping the rest of the bands in the row.

3. Continue with the rest of the bands, moving on to the centre row, and then to the right side.

4. When you get to the last peg use the hook to insert the extra white band through it. Tighten it around the bands on that hook with a slipknot before lifting off.

5. Use the hook to push through the row of bands to the inside of the beads. Push the beads through the hole to the bottom of the charm. This will make them look like wheels!

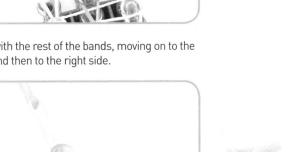

50. FLOWER POWER

Loom configuration: STAGGERED

You will need

12 white
6 yellow
1 pink
1 green (used for finishing)

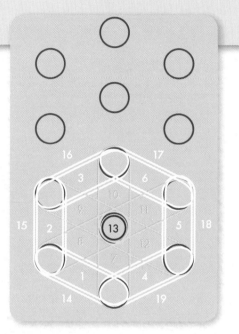

Place the loom with the arrows facing away from you, and lay the bands as per the diagram.

1. Turn the loom so the arrow faces toward you. Put your hook in the central peg, push back the topper band, and take the top yellow band to its original peg on the upper left-hand side.

2. Repeat this for the five remaining bands, working in an anticlockwise direction. Once you've looped all six bands, your topper band will be evenly suspended around the central peg.

3. Now, put your hook in the first central peg, take the second-to-bottom band, and loop it to its original peg on the left-hand side.

4. Put the hook inside the peg you finished on, take the bottom band, and loop it forward, to its original peg. Repeat once, to end on the top central peg.

5. Repeat steps 3 and 4 on the right-hand side, starting by taking the bottom band from inside the first central peg.

6. Put your hook through the last central peg, hook your green finishing band up through the peg, and then through itself, to create a slipknot.

7. Pull your flower off the loom. If petals are caught in the green finishing band, pinch the bands just below the slipknot and ease the knot open. Once it's open, thread it through the outer petals, and then re-slipknot it.

51. RAINBOW

Loom configuration: STAGGERED

You will need:

12 red

12 orange   12 purple

12 yellow   2 gold

12 green

12	24	**36**	48	60	72	**73**
11	23	**35**	47	59	71	
10	22	**34**	46	58	70	
9	21	**33**	45	57	69	
8	20	**32**	44	56	68	
7	19	**31**	43	55	67	
6	18	**30**	42	54	66	
5	17	**29**	41	53	65	
4	16	**28**	40	52	64	
3	15	**27**	39	51	63	
2	14	**26**	38	50	62	
1	13	**25**	37	49	61	

Place the loom with the arrows facing away from you, and lay bands on top of one another as per diagram. Don't forget topper band 73!

1. Turn the loom so the arrow is facing down towards you. Put your hook in the first peg on the right-hand side, push back the topper band, take the bottom red band, pull it up through the other bands, and loop forward to the next peg.

2. Put your hook in the second peg, hook the bottom red band, and loop forward. Keep looping the bottom red bands forward to the end of the loom. Be careful to pull them gently so they don't snap.

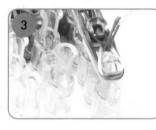

3. Go back to the first peg, push back the topper band, take the bottom orange band, pull it up through the other bands, and loop forward to the next peg.

4. Loop the orange bands to the end of the loom.

5. Repeat this process with the yellow, then the green, then the blue, and finally, the purple bands.

6. Then put your hook through the last peg in the chain, catch your gold finishing band, pull it up through, and create a slipknot with itself.

7. Pull your rainbow off the loom, and hopefully you'll find your pot of gold!

52. CACTUS

Loom configuration: 2 LOOMS, SQUARED

You will need

23 green
1 orange

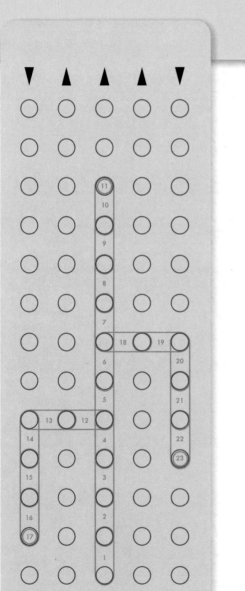

Turn the loom so that the arrow is facing away from you. Lay bands 1–23 according to the layout. Bands number 11, 17, and 23 will be topper bands. When you're finished laying out the bands, the one orange band will be left. This will be used later as a slipknot.

1. Turn the loom around so the middle arrow is facing you. Begin at band 23. Insert the hook into the peg to push back the topper band. Hook the bands beneath and loop forward to the peg it originated from. Loop all in that row, stopping after you loop band 18.

4. When you get to the last peg use the hook to insert the orange band through it.

2. Now go to band 17. Insert the hook into the peg to push the double topper band back and hook it onto the bands beneath. Pull that band up and off the peg and onto the peg where it originated. Loop all in that row, stopping after you loop band 12.

5. Tighten it around the bands on that hook with a slipknot before gently removing the charm from the loom.

3. Now go to band 11. Insert the hook into the peg to push back the topper band and hook the bands beneath. Pull that band up and onto the peg in front of it. Loop the rest of the bands.

CHAPTER 5
HOLIDAY FUN

There are some great projects out there for seasonal holidays, which are sure to get you in the festive spirit. Themed around some of the most popular celebrations in the calendar, these will give you something to look forward to all year round. They can be given as gifts to friends and family, or used as decorations for the occasion, and this range varies from easy to more complex. So relax, enjoy your holiday, and loom away!

53. BIRTHDAY GIFT

Loom configuration: SQUARED

You will need
14 clear yellow
13 turquoise

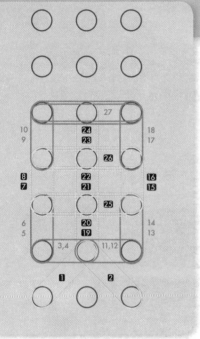

Place the loom with the arrows facing away from you, and lay the bands as per the diagram. Topper bands 25, 26, and 27 are wrapped around the pegs twice.

1. Turn the loom so the arrow faces towards you. Put your hook in the first left-hand peg, push back the topper band, and loop the bottom bands forward.

2. Repeat twice more in this row with the pairs of bands in front. Make sure your hook always goes inside the topper band.

3. Putting your hook in the peg you just finished on, take the bottom pair of bands and loop them to the middle peg.

4. Repeat steps 1–3 on the right-hand side.

5. Put your hook in the first central peg, push back the topper band, and loop the bottom pair of bands forward.

6. Repeat twice more in this row with the pairs of bands in front. Make sure your hook always goes inside the topper band.

7. Put your hook in the band you just finished on, take the second-to-bottom band, and loop it to its original peg on the upper left-hand side.

8. Repeat by taking the bottom band from the central peg to the upper right-hand side.

9. On the upper left-hand peg, hook the bottom end of the band up through itself to create a slipknot.

10. Repeat step 9 on the right-hand side. Gently pull your birthday gift off the loom.

54. VALENTINE'S HEART

Loom configuration: STAGGERED

You will need

33 red

1 gold

Place the loom with the arrows facing away from you, and lay the bands as per the diagram. Topper bands 32 and 33 are wrapped around the pegs twice, topper bands 30, 33, and 34 three times.

1. Turn the loom so the arrows are pointing towards you. Put your hook in the first left-hand peg, push back the topper band, take the top pair of bands diagonally to the fourth central peg from the top.

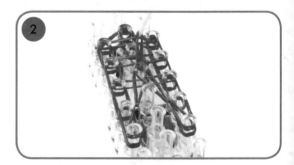

2. Repeat step 1 on the right-hand side. Then, putting your hook inside the peg you just looped to, take the bottom pair of bands and loop them forward.

3. Repeat, looping the next pair of bands forward.

4. Go back to the first left-hand peg, push back the topper band, take the pair of bands, and loop forward.

5. Continue looping the next five pairs of bands in this row, making sure to always hook from inside the topper bands. Note that the last band on the chain will be looped diagonally to the central row.

7. Put your hook inside the peg you just finished on, take the gold band from the bottom, loop forward and create a slipknot. Pull your heart off the loom and give to a special someone!

JSYK!

This project involves working with multiple bands which can be tricky, so work carefully to avoid bands snapping.

6. Repeat steps 4–5 on the right-hand side, so that all the red bands end on the same peg, second from the top in the central row.

55. EASTER BUNNY

Loom configuration: STAGGERED

You will need

47 white
2 gold
2 blue beads
1 pink bead

Place the loom with the arrows facing away from you and lay the bands as per the diagram. To get the pink bead in place, take your pair of gold bands, and thread them through the centre of the bead before stretching them between the pegs, in the position of bands 45 and 46. This will be the nose.

To get the blue beads in place, take your last white band, and thread it through the centre of the bead before stretching it between the pegs, in the position of band 48. Make sure your bead 'eyes' are evenly spaced. Bands 10 and 19 are wrapped twice around the pegs.

1. Turn the loom so the arrow is facing down towards you. We're going to start unconventionally by looping the ears first, which start on the top left-hand peg. Push back the topper band, put your hook to the side, and loop the bottom pair of bands towards you.

2. Continue looping toward you twice more with the next two pairs of bands. Make sure they always catch the previous band in their loops.

3. Repeat steps 1–2 on the right-hand side.

4. Now put your hook in the first used central peg, push back the topper band, hook the first pair of white bands, and loop it forward.

5. Continue looping the next three pairs of bands in the central row, making sure to always go inside the peg and topper band to catch the bottom bands.

6. Put your hook back in the first used central peg, push back the topper band, and take the top pair of bands diagonally to the upper left-hand side.

7. Loop four more pairs of bands in this row. The fourth band you hook will be looped diagonally to the upper right-hand side to the central row.

8. Repeat steps 6 and 7 on the right-hand side, starting back at the first used central peg.

9. Put your hook in the peg you just finished on, take the bottom white band and loop it forward. Pull the bottom end of the band up through the loop you just made to create a slipknot, and pull your Easter Bunny from the loom!

56. ALOHA NECKLACE

Loom configuration: SQUARED AND A MINI LOOM

You will need
250 green
90 orange
40 pink
40 yellow
1 O-clip

Place the loom with the arrows facing away from you; lay the bands as per the diagram. You are going to have to lay the loom like this another nine times, in order to make ten flowers and ten leaves, before attaching them to the necklace.

1. Turn the loom so the arrow is facing down towards you. We're going to start on the leaf. Put your hook through the first used central peg, push back the topper band, hook the first band, and loop it to its original peg on the left-hand side.

2. Continue looping the next three bands on the left, with the last one ending in the central row, making sure that the loose bands stay put.

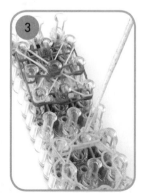

3. Repeat steps 1–2 on the right-hand side. Put your hook through the peg you just finished on, take the bottom band and loop forward, before pulling it though itself to create a slipknot. Pull off the loom – this is your first leaf.

4. Now we're going to loop the flower. Put your hook through the peg that is central to the square shape. Push the topper band with the back of your hook, catch the first band, and loop it back to its original peg on the upper left-hand side.

5. Repeat this process for the seven remaining bands, working in an anticlockwise direction. The cap band should now be evenly stretched around the central peg.

6. Put your hook through the first used central peg, hook the bottom band, and loop it to its original peg on the left-hand side.

7. Continue looping the next three bands on the left, with the last one ending in the central row.

8. Repeat steps 6–7 on the right-hand side to meet the other bands at the middle-top peg of the square. Put your hook through the peg you just finished on, take the bottom band and loop forward, before pulling it though itself to create a slipknot. Pull off the loom – this is your first flower.

9. Re-lay the loom and repeat steps 1–8 another nine times until you have a total of ten leaves and ten flowers.

10. We are now going to join them together by creating a chain on the Mini Loom. Take a single green band, wrap it twice around the Mini Loom, and make a chain using another three green bands, following the instructions on page 9. Then, instead of using a fifth green band, take the end of the green slipknot from your first leaf, and loop that in the chain instead.

11. Loop another four green bands, before using the slipknot from your first flower in the chain.

12. Keep extending the chain in this way by four bands at a time, before adding in either a leaf or flower, until all your leaves and flowers are part of the chain.

13. Now, attach the two ends of the last band with an O-clip, before pulling the chain off the Mini Loom and attaching the other end to the O-clip, too. Aloha!

57. HALLOWEEN SPIDER

Loom configuration: STAGGERED

You will need

124 dark purple
2 green
2 black beads

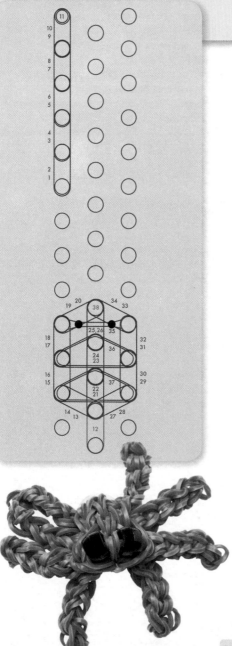

Place the loom with the arrows facing away from you and lay the bands as per the diagram. Bands 1–11 will have to be placed a total of eight times to create your spider's legs. Topper bands 11 and 38 are wrapped four times around the peg. Topper bands 36 and 37 are wrapped twice. Thread band 35 through two beads before stretching between the pegs.

1. Turn the loom so the arrow is facing down towards you. Put your hook in the first right-hand peg, push back the cap band, hook the top pair of bands, and loop forward.

2. Continue to loop forward the next four pairs of bands in the row, always going inside the cap band to loop them. Put your hook in the last peg in the chain and pull it off the loom.

3. Slide your bands off the hook and position this leg on the second peg down on the left-hand side.

4. Re-lay the loom with bands 1–11 and repeat steps 1–2 seven more times, positioning one leg on the third peg down, and two legs on the fourth peg down on the left-hand side. Repeat this positioning on the right.

5. Put your hook in the first central peg, push back the cap band, hook the top pair of bands, and loop diagonally to the left-hand row.

6. Continue looping forward the next two pairs of bands in this row. The last pair will be looped diagonally to the upper central peg, always going inside the cap band to loop them.

7. Put your hook back in the first central peg, push back the cap band, hook the next pair of bands down, and loop them forward.

8. Continue looping forward the next two pairs of bands in this row.

9. Repeat steps 5 and 6 on the right-hand side.

10. Put your hook in the peg you just finished on, reach down, catch the bottom green band, and loop it forward.

11. Loop the bottom end of the band up through the middle of itself, pulling it into a slipknot.

58. FIREWORKS NECKLACE

Loom configuration: 2 LOOMS ATTACHED SIDE BY SIDE, SQUARED, PLUS MINI LOOM

You will need

59 silver	6 purple
6 white	6 beads,
6 yellow	the shinier
6 orange	the better!
6 pink	1 O-clip

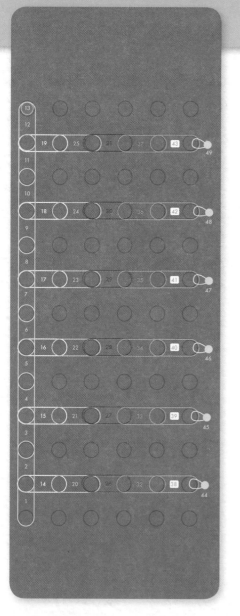

Place the loom with the arrows facing away from you; lay the bands as per the diagram. To get the beads in place, take a single silver band, thread it through the bead, then stretch both ends of it onto the peg.

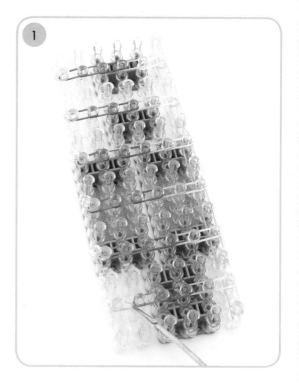

1. Turn the loom so the arrow is facing down towards you. Place your hook through the second peg up on the left, and loop the bottom band to its original peg, on the right-hand side.

2. Continue to loop the remaining four bands in the chain to the right-hand side.

122

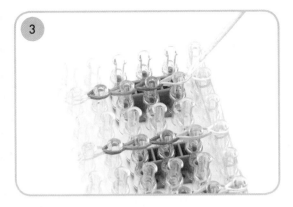

3. Continue looping the next five horizontal chains from left to right, ending each one in the right-hand row.

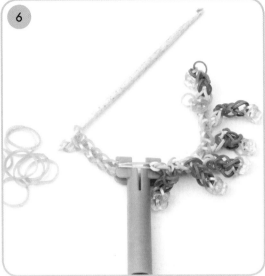

6. When you get to the end of the loom, put your hook through both ends of the last band and pull off the loom. Stretch these two band ends over your Mini Loom, and extend by 20 bands (see page 9 for help). Then, attach the last band ends with an O-Clip.

7. Now stretch the other end of the chain over the Mini Loom, and extend this side by a further 20 bands, before sliding the ends into the O-clip.

4. Put your hook through the first peg in the right-hand row, push back the topper band, take the bottom band and loop forward.

5. Continue looping the next 11 bands in the chain along the right-hand row, making sure you only catch the band that you require.

59. SNOWFLAKE

Loom configuration: STAGGERED

You will need

168 clear blue

31 silver

6 C-clips

Place the loom with the arrows facing away from you, and lay the bands as per the diagram, paying particular attention to the numbers. Topper band 34 is wrapped around the peg twice, while topper bands 29–33 are wrapped three times around their pegs. You will have to lay the loom like this a total of six times, to make six icicles.

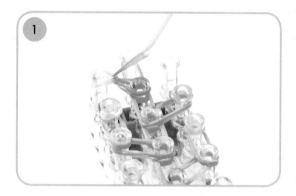

1. Turn the loom so the arrow is facing down toward you. Put your hook in the top left-hand peg, push back the topper band, hook the bottom pair of bands, and loop them diagonally back to their original peg, to the lower right-hand side, in the central row.

2. Put your hook in the second peg down on the right-hand side, push back the topper band, hook the bottom pair of bands, and loop them diagonally back to their original peg, to the lower left-hand side, in the central row.

5. Repeat steps 3 and 4 twice, starting first at the third peg down on the right and then the fourth down on the left. Now put your hook in the first used central peg. Push back the topper band, take the bottom pair of bands, and loop forward.

6. Continue looping the next five pairs of bands forward, from inside the pegs.

3. Put your hook in the second peg down on the left-hand side, hook the bottom pair of bands, and link them down towards you.

7. Once you get to the end of the loom, put your hook in the peg, slide the bands on to it and attach them with a C-clip, before pulling your first icicle off the loom.

4. Then, starting at the peg you just looped to, take the bottom pair of bands and loop them diagonally back to their original peg, to the lower right-hand side, in the central row.

8. Re-lay your loom with bands 1–33. Stretch the topper band from your first icicle in place of band 34, and repeat steps 1–7. Then repeat steps 1–8 four more times to make six icicles, all attached to the same topper band, to create a perfect snowflake.

60. CHRISTMAS STOCKING

Loom configuration: SQUARED

You will need

48 red

20 white

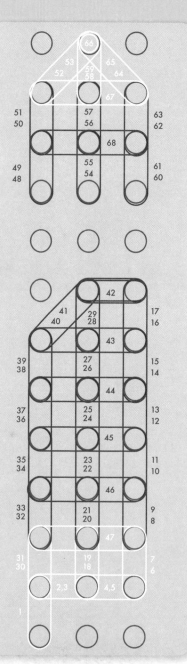

Place the loom with the arrows facing away from you and lay the bands as per the diagram. Topper band 66 is wrapped four times around the peg. Topper band 42 is wrapped twice between the pegs. All other horizontal bands are wrapped just once.

1. Turn the loom so the arrow is facing down towards you. Start by making the toe. Put your hook in the first central peg, push back the topper band, hook the top pair of bands, and loop them diagonally to the upper left-hand side.

2. Putting your hook in the peg you just finished on, hook the bottom pair of bands forward, making sure you go inside the topper band.

3. Go back to the first central peg and repeat steps 1 and 2, once in the central row and then in the right-hand row.

4. Put your hook in the fourth peg up on the right-hand side, and slide the bands onto it. Repeat the process on the fourth central and left-hand pegs, so you have three sets of looped bands on your hook. Pull your 'toe' off the loom.

10. Now put your hook in the sixth peg up from the bottom on the left-hand side, take the very bottom pair of bands from the inside of the peg, and loop forward.

5. We are now going to attach the toe to the rest of the sock. Go to the eighth peg up from the bottom of the left-hand side, and slide the first set of bands off your hook onto the peg.

11. Repeat five times more, being very careful to make sure all the other bands stay on their pegs. It will get quite tight when you are pulling the bottom bands, so be gentle. When you get to the end of the chain in this row, put your hook inside the last peg, take the bottom pair of bands, and loop to the right.

6. Slide the second set of bands off your hook and onto the seventh peg up from the bottom on the left-hand side, and the third set of bands onto the sixth peg up from the bottom on the left-hand side.

12. At the peg you just looped to, take the bottom pair of bands and loop them right, too.

7. Put your hook in the central sixth peg up from the bottom, push back the topper band, hook the first pair of bands, and loop them diagonally to the upper right-hand side.

8. Put your hook in the peg you just finished on, hook the bottom pair of bands and loop forward, and continue with the next four pairs of bands in the chain.

13. Put your hook in the peg you just looped to, take the bottom band, and loop it forward. Now hook the bottom end of it off the peg and through the loop you just made to create a slipknot.

9. Go back to the sixth central peg up from the bottom, push back the topper band, hook the bottom pair of bands, and loop them forward. Continue looping the next five pairs of bands in the chain.

14. Ease your stocking off the loom and wait for Santa!

RESOURCES

UK

LOOM BANDING EQUIPMENT

ABC Zone: abczone.co.uk
Amazon: amazon.co.uk
Argos: argos.co.uk
Claire's: claires.co.uk
eBay: ebay.co.uk
The Entertainer: thetoyshop.com
Smyth's: smythstoys.com
Tesco: tesco.com
Toys 'R' Us: toysrus.co.uk
Toymaster: toymastershop.co.uk
The Works: theworks.co.uk

CRAFT, HABERDASHERY AND JEWELLERYRY

Hobbycraft: hobbycraft.co.uk
John Lewis: johnlewis.com
Etsy: etsy.com

US

LOOM BANDING EQUIPMENT

Michael's: michaels.com
Learning Express: learningexpress.com
J and R: jr.com
Amazon: amazon.com
eBay: ebay.com

CRAFT, HABERDASHERY AND JEWELLERY

Create for Less: createforless.com
Jewelry Supply: jewelrysupply.com
Jemco: jemcousa.com
Auntie's Beads: auntiesbeads.com
M & J Trimming: mjtrim.com
Etsy: etsy.com